60

FARRAR
STRAUS
GIROUX

T0057948

❖❖ Praise for *The Solitude of Self* ❖❖

"*Wow.* Not only does Vivian Gornick transform Elizabeth Cady Stanton from a name in a Women's Studies class into a flesh-and-blood lady, she convinced me that feminism itself is as American as apple pie."
—Jennifer Baumgardner, coauthor of
Manifesta: Young Women, Feminism, and the Future

"There's a curious excitement that moves through Vivian Gornick's thoughts about Elizabeth Cady Stanton. 'Suffrage,' she writes, 'was the university in which [Stanton's] feeling intelligence was now enrolled.' And one suspects it's Gornick's too. Not the movement for the vote, but the deeper wrestling with the obstacles to equality—religion, for example, and the solitude of the self. These were Stanton's contributions to radical feminism, and Gornick rescues them from that brilliant nineteenth-century oratory." —Carol Brightman, author of *Writing Dangerously: Mary McCarthy and Her World*

"A powerful meditation that is at once informative and moving."
—Martin Duberman, author of *Paul Robeson: A Biography*

"In heartfelt and toughminded prose, Vivian Gornick illuminates the fearless intellect of Elizabeth Cady Stanton, the first American feminist to grasp the essential truth that an independent woman must free herself from worship of all man-made institutions—including those purporting to speak for God. We all stand today on the shoulders of this giant."
—Susan Jacoby, author of *Freethinkers: A History of American Secularism*

"In this vivid triumph of biography and cultural criticism, Vivian Gornick discovers at the root of Elizabeth Cady Stanton's polemic a sustaining and deeply American philosophy of the self. Leading us into the thinking of this great feminist, Gornick offers a way to embrace the solitude that is, for every thinking human being, the fiercest attachment of all."

—Honor Moore, author of *The White Blackbird: A Life of the Painter Margarett Sargent by Her Granddaughter*

"The real story of this illuminating study is not only that of a brave American's fight for equality of the sexes, but of the human yearning to be truly free, and of the lonely, fearful struggle with society, and even with oneself, that such a noble goal entails."

—Ronald Steel, author of *Walter Lippmann and the American Century*

"In this wonderful biographical essay, Vivian Gornick notes that Mary Wollstonecraft and Simone de Beauvoir each distilled her passion and philosophy into one major book about and for women. But their nineteenth-century peer, Elizabeth Cady Stanton, whose medium was the political speech, wrote no single beacon text, no summa. So Gornick has done it for her. Better late than never—although in the ongoing story of feminism this 'essence of Stanton' is, in fact, alas, early."

—Elisabeth Young-Bruehl, author of *Hannah Arendt: For Love of the World*

VIVIAN GORNICK

The Solitude of Self

Vivian Gornick's books include *Fierce Attachments, Approaching Eye Level, The End of the Novel of Love,* and *The Situation and the Story.* She lives in New York City.

Also by Vivian Gornick

The Situation and the Story

The End of the Novel of Love

Approaching Eye Level

Fierce Attachments

THE SOLITUDE OF SELF

THE
SOLITUDE OF SELF

Thinking About Elizabeth Cady Stanton

Vivian Gornick

FARRAR, STRAUS AND GIROUX

NEW YORK

FARRAR, STRAUS AND GIROUX
18 West 18th Street, New York 10011

Printed in the United States of America
Published in 2005 by Farrar, Straus and Giroux
First paperback edition, 2006

The Library of Congress has cataloged the hardcover edition as follows:
Gornick, Vivian.
The solitude of self : thinking about Elizabeth Cady Stanton / Vivian Gornick.— 1st ed.
    p. cm.
Includes bibliographical references.
ISBN-13: 978-0-374-29954-5
ISBN-10: 0-374-29954-4 (hardcover : alk. paper)
I. Stanton, Elizabeth Cady, 1815–1902. 2. Women's rights. I. Title.

HQ1413.S67G67   2005
305.42'092—dc22

                                                                    2004028476

Paperback ISBN-13: 978-0-374-53056-3
Paperback ISBN-10: 0-374-53056-4

Designed by Patrice Sheridan

www.fsgbooks.com

This book is dedicated to Ellen Carol DuBois

and to

Ann D. Gordon

and all who labor with her on the magisterial six-volume

production of

The Selected Papers of Elizabeth Cady Stanton and Susan B. Anthony

CONTENTS

CHAPTER I

1840: To Begin With   3

CHAPTER II

1848: A Radical Among Radicals   29

CHAPTER III

1867: We Are Alone   91

CHAPTER IV

1894–2004: From There to Here   116

Bibliographical Note   133

THE SOLITUDE OF SELF

1840
TO BEGIN WITH

ONE AFTERNOON IN JANUARY OF 1892, in a packed convention hall in Washington, D.C., a seventy-six-year-old woman rose from her seat with difficulty to address the assembled audience. She was short and very fat, dressed from neck to ankle in black silk, possessed of a clear complexion, bright blue eyes, and a headful of famously thick white curls. She could have posed as "grandmotherly Americana" except that her features were stamped with an excess of complicated character (open, haughty, warm, aloof), and over the whole of her face there played a restless intelligence upon which one might well hesitate to inflict boredom.

The woman's name was Elizabeth Cady Stanton. The occasion was the third annual meeting of the newly formed National American Woman Suffrage Association. The title alone made her sigh. So much history behind it, so much anger and regret. More than twenty years before, in the wake of the Civil War, the women's rights movement, caught up in one of the worst quarrels in history over universal suffrage, had split into two associations—the National and the

American. Now, two years before this moment, it had been agreed among the original antagonists—Stanton herself; her comrade in arms, Susan B. Anthony; and their adversary, Lucy Stone—that the two groups would close the split, and reunite. Stanton had then, uneasily, become the association's first president. She knew even as she campaigned for the post that vanity alone was driving her, as she was still contemptuous of Lucy Stone and her followers, and deeply at odds with the conservatism of the younger feminists now in the ascendancy in both associations. These women had, in her view, narrowed the large, visionary character of women's rights she so passionately loved down to the kind of single-issue, nuts-and-bolts politics she had come to deplore. She could understand the frustration that had led them to this pragmatism—after all, it was now forty years that they'd been struggling to win the vote—but she deplored it nonetheless. She had traveled too far in her mind to backtrack along *this* road.

She herself had begun with the same single-minded passion for suffrage, burning in her since 1840, when she had first understood that in the eyes of the world she was "only a woman"; but the long years of failure—and this set her well apart from most of her generation of feminists—had fed a radicalism in her that had kept her thoughts moving around the stubborn, unyielding urge toward social equality that drove the reformers of her time. From suffrage to marriage to education to divorce to organized religion—in the name of women's rights she had examined each, always asking: How has *this* arrangement come about? For whose benefit, and to whose detriment, are these laws and customs in place? What underlying purpose do they serve? What is *actually* going on here? As these questions had taken hold of her, her attention had deepened and turned ever more thoughtful; that is, ever more inward. In the end, women's rights had

become an instrument of illumination; attained metaphoric proper-
ties; made her understand something profound about the human
condition.

She looked out at the few thousand faces gathered before her.
Most of them she was seeing for the first time, but many she had
been gazing at for more than forty years. They were all there: the talented organizers, the industrious drones, the narrowly intelligent
polemicists. They looked back at her. Not one face, familiar or
strange, shone with expectation; all seemed guarded or openly apprehensive. She knew what they were wondering: What on earth is going to come out of her mouth *now*? It had often been this way—her
audience braced for at least one shocker—but in the old days (and
for many, many years before this moment) the shocks had been salu-
tary. She had spoken aloud what most of them had wanted to have
said—by someone other than themselves. Those who had *not* wanted
to hear what she had to say had then been in the minority. Now, she
knew for certain, the proportions were reversed. She could smell it
in the air, very nearly she could taste it. The division between herself
and the people in this room was crucial. Whereas once the atmosphere glowed with solidarity, it now sparked with antagonism. She
had decided to step down from the presidency. This would be her
last public speech as head of the woman suffrage movement.

Stanton had been feeling this separation between herself and her
beloved movement for a very long time. It had induced in her a terrible loneliness, unlike any that she had ever known. The loneliness
had become an experience that sent her thoughts driving directly at
the pain. There she had found herself staring, with sorrow and interest, into a sense of isolation that had proved revelatory. As she
traveled deeper into her own solitary state, she came to understand
viscerally what she had before considered only with her reasoning.

She had always known that the bonds of human connection are frag-
ile, subject to time, circumstance, and the mystery of slowly altering
sympathies, but she had never before doubted that making connection was the norm; it represented a defining trait: the need for
intimacy. To make connection was to be in a state of normality.
Conversely, to find oneself alone, an isolate without steady or permanent attachment, was—and this, too, she had never doubted—to
lay oneself open to the one thing people were pathologically ashamed
of being charged with: abnormality. Now, suddenly, it flashed on her
that it was loneliness that was the norm. Connection was an ideal:
the exception, not the rule, in the human condition.

Much in her life might have contributed to this insight—a disappointing marriage, friendships that had run their course, a passion
for motherhood that had also run its course—but more than any of
these experiences it was this one, the irreversible separateness she
now felt within the ranks of her own movement, that supplied the
emotional proof: not only is no attachment reliably enduring, but
when the most intimate and solid-seeming are dissolved, we experience a sense of aloneness that, surprisingly, is not alien; it is almost
as though we feel ourselves returned to some earlier condition. It
strikes us then—and this was the revelation—that we are *embarrassed*
by the "return." It marks us, in our own eyes, as failures at doing life.
We shrink from confiding the embarrassment to a living soul, even
the nearest of intimates. The reticence creates a distance between
ourselves and all others. Inside the distance, in the innermost being,
we remain solitary. As we grow older, the solitariness increases. Stanton looked hard at what she was seeing, and she thought, How
unspeakable, then, that worldly arrangements should contribute to
the forlornness of one's natural state! Politics is meant to mitigate
the misery to which the human condition consigns us, not add to it.

The long, rich devotion to women's rights had given her many extraordinary insights, though none more powerful than this one. She turned to her manuscript. The title page read "The Solitude of Self." She began to speak.

The thing that she wanted her audience to consider, she said, was the individuality of a human being: that which Protestant American culture held as a first value. In one sense, the idea of the individual is a declaration of proud independence; in another, it is the recognition that we are, in fact, a world of Robinson Crusoes, each of us alone on the island of life:

> No matter how much women prefer to lean, to be protected and supported, nor how much men desire to have them do so, they must make the voyage of life alone, and for safety in an emergency, they must know something of the laws of navigation. To guide our own craft, we must be captain, pilot, engineer; with chart and compass to stand at the wheel; to watch the winds and waves, and know when to take in the sail, and to read the signs in the firmament over all. It matters not whether the solitary voyager is man or woman; nature, having endowed them equally, leaves them to their own skill and judgment in the hour of danger, and, if not equal to the occasion, alike they perish.

She realized that to the greatest degree the solitude is self-created, the result of being locked from birth into a psychology of shame: "Our most bitter disappointments, our brightest hopes and ambitions, are known only to ourselves . . . there is something of every passion, in every situation, we conceal . . . We ask no sympathy from others in the anxiety and agony of a broken friendship or shattered love. When death sunders our nearest ties, alone we sit in the shadow of our affliction. Alike amid the greatest triumphs and darkest tragedies of life, we walk alone." It is precisely *because* this is the reality of our nature, she continues, that we are compelled to create a society that will help us fight the worst in ourselves. To deny *anyone* the tools of survival—that is, the power to act—is criminal. One of these tools, surely, is political liberty. The strongest reason that she, Stanton, knew for giving women every means of enlarging their sphere of action is the ultimate solitariness of every life. And it is from this perspective that she now speaks directly to the consequence of withholding the rights of citizens who are women:

> The talk of sheltering woman from the fierce storms of life is the sheerest mockery, for they beat on her from every point of the compass, just as they do on man, and with more fatal results, for he has been trained to protect himself, to resist, and to conquer. Such are the facts in human experience . . . rich and poor, intelligent and ignorant, wise and foolish, virtuous and vicious, man and woman; it is ever the same, each soul must depend wholly on itself . . . [I]n the long, weary march, each one walks alone . . .
>
> [This] is a solitude which each and every one of us has always carried with him, more inaccessible than the ice-cold mountains, more profound than the midnight sea; the solitude of self. Our inner being which we call ourself, no eye nor touch of man or angel has ever pierced . . . Such is individual life. Who, I ask you, can take, dare take on himself the rights, the duties, the responsibilities of another human soul?

She read these words into a silent room. No one clapped, no one spoke. Not because the audience, as when Lincoln delivered the Gettysburg Address, was profoundly moved, but because a voice speaking existential truth was not, at this politically practical moment, wanted. It was, however, a very American speech that she had given, one that any of the original Revolutionaries might have made, bent as he would have been on forcing politics to reflect a New World insistence that equality would let one grow a self strong enough and independent enough to do battle with life's irreducible starkness. This was how Americans arrived at eloquence: insisting on *more* democracy. Not another American feminist had ever, until that moment in 1892, placed the cause of women's rights so squarely at the center of such perceptions.

ELIZABETH CADY STANTON is the American visionary thinker of the nineteenth century equal in intellectual stature to the two feminist greats who preceded and followed her: Mary Wollstonecraft and Simone de Beauvoir. Like them, she had the philosophical cast of mind large enough to see the thing whole, to grasp with radical speed the immensity that women's rights addressed. Each of these women—Wollstonecraft, Stanton, Beauvoir—had been an ardent partisan of a powerful intellectual movement—the Enlightenment, abolitionism, existentialism—and the contribution that each made to feminist understanding turned, appropriately enough, on an application of the central insight of the movement to which she had been devoted. Wollstonecraft urged passionately that women become rational beings; Stanton that every woman exercise governance over her own inviolable self; Beauvoir that women cease to be Other (that is, become the central actor in their own lives).

Stanton differed from the other two in that each of them wrote a single famous-making book at white heat in a comparatively short time—*Vindication of the Rights of Woman* over a period of a few weeks, *The Second Sex* over a few years—while she, Stanton, lived within the embrace of feminist thought for half a century, thinking the matter out decade by decade, provocation by provocation, through a series of speeches, letters, and essays that demonstrate the preoccupation with revolutionary republicanism that led her steadily toward an ever more existential view of the human condition.

It was the promise of the democracy outraged that was working in her, flaring as brightly at the end of her political life as at the beginning. Behind that enduring slow burn lies the whole strength of American liberationist movements. It is what makes them American. That unyielding sense of outrage—the one that's experienced when one realizes the democracy is being held in check by virtue of class, race, or sex—is serious in this country, serious and lasting. It is responsible for the great civil rights movements of our own time. Certainly it is responsible for the fact that modern feminism has repeatedly taken root here and not elsewhere, even though its intellectual beginnings can be traced to the work of brilliant Europeans. Much as the Europeans might burn over their second-class status, it was impossible for them—from Wollstonecraft's generation to Beauvoir's—to give up their longing for inclusion in the world as men have made it. This longing has always bound them to a dividedness of will that is politically crippling. The Americans, on the other hand, were moved to harden their hearts against the romantic pull of the world as it is, and concentrate on the denial of what is promised them by right of birth—not birth into the world, birth into the American democracy. That concentration is the poetry of Elizabeth Stanton's political existence: it multiplied her insight, deepened her thought, clarified her spirit. Had she written "the book" we would be reading her today instead of John Stuart Mill on the subjection of women. As it is, she left public life with that final address—"The Solitude of Self"—its long shadows casting back to Plato, forward to our own day. Hers was the American contribution, and it goes far to explain why feminism as a liberation movement has flourished here as nowhere else in the Western world, rising up repeatedly every fifty years or so—never reversing itself, never completing itself—always arriving out of a passion of original discovery that is both painful and stirring. When it was my turn to realize that in the eyes of the world I was only a woman, Elizabeth Stanton's was the voice that spoke most clearly to me across the intervening century.

IN NOVEMBER OF 1970, an editor at *The Village Voice* asked me to go out and investigate women's libbers.

"What's that?" I asked.

A week later I was a convert.

First, I met Ti-Grace Atkinson, Kate Millett, and Shulamith Firestone; next, Phyllis Chesler, Ellen Willis, and Alix Kates Shulman. They were all talking at once, and I heard every word each of them spoke. Or, rather, it was that I must have heard them all saying the same thing, because I came away from that week branded by a single thought. It was this: the idea that men by nature take their brains seriously and women by nature do not is a belief, not an inborn reality—an idea that serves the culture, and from it our entire lives follow. Simple, really. And surely this had already been said. How was it that I seemed never to have heard it before? And why was I hearing it now? A question that cannot be answered. It remains one of life's great mysteries, the matter of political readiness; that moment when the elements of dissatisfaction in a culture are sufficiently fused to achieve a critical mass. If you are one who responds to the moment you can never really explain it, you can only describe what it felt like.

Now, in 1970, awake and asleep, a review of my life *as a woman* kept repeating itself like a broken record going round and round inside my head. Again and again, I rehearsed—in snatched phrases, fleeting images, half sentences—that which I had grown up accepting as normal and now experienced as alien. As though waking from a dream, I found myself daily uncovering evidence of a culture within that had been hidden, so to speak, in plain sight. I was, suddenly, a candidate for lost memory.

I *remembered* my mother and my aunt beaming when, as a child, I performed intellectually, at the same time telling me that I'd soon have to put a lid on it, since no man wants a woman to be that smart and love is the most important thing in a woman's life. I could see myself nodding, as though taking instruction in the laws of the universe.

I *remembered* a classmate at City College taunting me with Aristotle, repeating the philosopher's assertion that women are the first deviation in nature—a deformity, an infertile male—and me responding hotly, but in the style of Katharine Hepburn sparring with Spencer Tracy, both of whom, beneath all the splendid speeches, also knew that love is the most important thing in a woman's life.

I *remembered* an eminent physicist telling me that women could be good scientists but not great scientists; it had to do with a crucial difference in the nervous system.

I *remembered* my young husband and me talking for hours about what we would do with the future, both clearly taking it for granted that his life was to be our life.

I *remembered* an English Department chairman telling me, in the early sixties, that women did not receive tenure at his school, and me murmuring, "Of course" without surprise or complaint.

I *remembered* an analyst saying to me in that same decade, "You don't want to *marry* the great man, you want to *be* the great man," as though he had discovered my dirty little secret, and I staring speechlessly at him: guilty as charged.

Now I found myself thinking: Who on earth *says* such things to a human being whom the speaker considers as real as he is to himself? Who tells another person, whom you believe made in the same image as you, that the wish to experience one's own finite self to the fullest is unnatural? Who thinks it acceptable that a set of needs described as essential to *any*one's humanity be considered necessary for some but not for others? Who indeed.

Everything about this moment had the far-reaching power of conversion. I remember writing my first feminist piece as though I'd been struck by religious lightning. What a drama it was, seeing with new sight what one had been looking at all of one's life—to look and to see, "a two fold action," as the poet Charles Bernstein puts it—to realize that well into the final half of the twentieth century women *still* did not take their brains seriously. It struck me forcibly in 1970 that universal culture remained posited on the unspoken understanding that no man, and all too few women, would challenge the immutability of second-class status for women. Nothing, we now saw—and this was electrifying—had ever been expected of us: not by "them," not by ourselves.

The words had never before come into my head. It was the last description on earth I would have applied to myself: second-class citizen. What had such a phrase to do with *me*? Everything, as it turned out. I had always thought I knew well enough what it meant to be seen as "other"—I had, after all, grown up the child of Jewish working-class immigrants in a middle-class, Christian country governed by the educated and the native-born—but these problematic elements of identity had, at this time in this place, proven not to be written in stone; and in 1970 in New York City they seemed as nothing compared with what I now perceived to be an unalterable stigma of birth. I looked and I saw: I had been born into the wrong sex. The world would have to change radically before *that* would stop mattering. How unreal, I thought, I have been to myself! All these years, going along with a headful of dreamy plans to "find myself," "become myself," "exercise the freedom of an earned will." Suddenly, the words sounded unbearably foolish in my own ears. The naivete! To have never before understood the external limits placed upon any journey into, and then out of, the self that might be undertaken by a person who is a woman.

The light was blinding, and then illuminating—and, I must say, the illumination was an astonishing comfort. I woke up with it, danced through the day with it, fell asleep smiling with it. I became impervious: the slings and arrows of daily fortune could not make a dent in me. Life felt good then. I had insight, and I had company. I stood in the middle of my own experience, turning and turning. In every direction I saw a roomful of women, also turning and turning.

That is a moment of joy, when a sufficiently large number of people are galvanized by a social explanation of how their lives have taken shape and are gathered together in the same place at the same time, meeting again and again in restaurants, lecture halls, and apartments for the pleasure of elaborating the insight and repeating the analysis. It is the joy of revolutionary politics, and it was ours. To be a feminist in the early 1970s—bliss was it in that dawn, to be alive. Not an I-love-you in the world could touch it. We lived then, all of us, inside the loose embrace of feminism: there was no other place to be, except with each other. I thought I would spend the rest of my life there. What we today see in our hundreds, I was convinced, will tomorrow surely be seen by thousands, and the day after that by millions. How could it be otherwise? Only people of serious ill will, or intellectual deficiency, or downright political greed would oppose the obvious. And, after all, how many of *them* could there be?

That our "obvious" truth would raise monumental anxieties in women and men alike, anxieties of the kind that throw people back on fears of a primitive order—this did not occur to us. When our point was not only not readily taken but violently disputed, both to the left and to the right, by conservatives and liberals alike, we were shocked. Shocked, and re-enforced. Opposition to the cause made jailhouse lawyers of us all. The need to justify ourselves required more explanation, more explanation required more thought, more thought made philosophical human beings out of countless women who might not otherwise have held so high a regard for the virtue of seeing things whole. And thus our numbers swelled.

Looking back on those visionary years, what I find most remarkable is the swiftness with which the course of thought among feminists widened and deepened. Almost from the beginning, the movement was philosophical in its nature, existential in its grasp. Yes, equal pay for equal work. Yes, pass the ERA. Yes, legal abortion and an end to job discrimination. But, at the same time, and surrounding all this down-to-earth politicking, was an immeasurably larger insight within which the politicalness of life was being understood as one of the great metaphors of organized existence. One feminist perspective after another—from psychologists, historians, political scientists, and literary critics—seemed to be addressing the whole of the human condition in its analysis of the insecurity and defensiveness behind the need, as Virginia Woolf had put it, to agree that women would live a half life in order that men might gain the courage to pursue a whole one. The agreement provided the stamina necessary to sustain without derangement the suspicion that one was, indeed, alone in the universe. A profound recognition of the fear of human loneliness *as a motive force* began to prevail among those of us who cared to think of it.

I hardly knew who Elizabeth Cady Stanton was—a nineteenth-century suffragist? a friend of Susan B. Anthony's?—when, sometime in that crucial decade, a feminist put into my hands "The Solitude of Self." I could not know then what this speech meant in her life, or in our history, but it was not hard to experience, with startling immediacy, the power of her prose or the modernity of her insight. I can still remember thinking with excitement and gratitude, as I read her words for the first time, eighty years after they were written, "We are beginning where she left off."

Reading Elizabeth Stanton in the seventies made me feel on my skin the shock of realizing how slowly (how grudgingly!) politics in the modern world has actually moved, over these past hundreds of years, to include unwanted classes of being in the much-vaunted devotion to egalitarianism. The word "outsider" deepened for me: its meaning and its destiny. The recognition, of an irreducible humanity from which I had not previously imagined myself excluded but now saw that I *was*, stunned me. It was this recognition that was burning itself into definition as I walked my own floor, reading Stanton, and it was through her fifty-year devotion that I began to develop an altogether new appreciation (familiar from a leftwing childhood) of taking "the long view."

I had known that the kaleidoscope of my experience was being shaken; that all the same pieces would still be there, only now surrounded by a new space, forming a new design—one I thought had not been seen before. Now, I saw that my new design was *old.* So old! Elizabeth Stanton had looked at it more than a hundred years before me, and had described it in the same words that I was now speaking, using the same examples, staring into the same historical void, feeling the same thin air thicken with the same anger and, more important, the same scared wonder. I realized how repeatedly, throughout modern history, this stunned awakening had taken place among women, and in how absolutely *similar* a set of words and phrases—from the late Enlightenment to this late-twentieth-century moment—it had been experienced. I didn't know whether to laugh or cry, feel energized or depleted, sprout wings of hope or curl up in terminal depression. In truth, I thought, it isn't over till it's over—and until it *is* over, each time around, *things look pretty much the same.* I knew that Stanton had stood where I was now standing, and I knew what she had done when she had seen that *she* was standing where others had stood before. I realized that I had no choice in the matter, either.

SHE WAS BORN IN 1815, in upstate New York, into a rich, conservative, socially connected family. Her father was a distinguished jurist with a taste for politics—he both practiced and taught law and was, at various times, a New York state assemblyman, a congressman, and a state supreme court judge. Her mother was a Livingston—the daughter of a Revolutionary War hero—with family connections that included Beekmans, Schuylers, and Van Rensselaers. Both parents were proud, principled, and Calvinist.

Ten children were born to the Cadys, of whom only five (Tryphena, Harriet, Catherine, Margaret, and Elizabeth) lived past the age of twenty: all girls. Of the five, three married their father's law students, one married a businessman, and those four lived conventional women's lives. Only Elizabeth emerged a radically serious person possessed of high spirits, some intellectual genius, and a re-markably intact ego that gave her more than enough nerve to honor what would turn out to be a ruling love of self-definition. The girl, and then the woman, who evolved out of these excellent traits of hu-man endowment was brilliant, rowdy, cheerful; caustic and curious; intellectually headlong and abidingly autocratic: she always knew where *she* came from. In time, the intellect gave her the joy of steady thought, the spirit made her regard social equality as a burning ne-cessity, and the lifelong sense of superiority forced her to struggle with a reckless disposition to scorn and dismiss. Beneath the grand-motherly image that overwhelmed her body in early middle age, and lasted throughout her long years, was a strong-willed, high-tempered young woman who faced all comers until she was eighty-five with her hands on her hips, her head tilted back, and her eyes narrowed skep-tically against the boring, the stupid, the uneducated.

These character-building teeth were cut on the contradiction (most alive inside her own adored father) between the pleasure of liberal reasoning on the one hand, and the repressiveness of old-time religion on the other: a contradiction that brought young Elizabeth to the edge quite early. In the Cady household, as in innumerable American homes at the time when she was growing up, there pre-vailed an unreconstructed Presbyterianism that posited original sin as one given, and the ever-present threat of an eternity spent in hell as another. It is hard to overstate the religious cast of this culture. In 1800, the rhetoric of Christianity informed the dailiness of Ameri-can life, all popular notions of virtue were visibly bound up with a Christian definition of moral obligation, thousands of young men routinely contemplated a life in the church, and in colleges and uni-versities religious thought and practice were thoroughly intermin-gled with every kind of intellectual inquiry. The idiom of religious belief—whether embraced, rebelled against, or grappled with—was the one through which men and women were most likely to come up against themselves.

Elizabeth—bold, witty, dramatically high-spirited—naturally took right into herself the anxieties produced both in church and at home by the routine admonition that we are born "sinners in the hands of an angry god"; they gave her nightmares, and they threw her into the kind of angry depression that an imaginative child who *knows* that she is bound for hell is likely to suffer. In her early teens she came close to the inevitable mental breakdown, from which she recovered a nonbeliever—that is, a serious nonbeliever. Many others growing up inside the same orthodox Calvinism—the children of the famous Beecher family, for instance, the one that included Harriet the writer and Henry the preacher—experienced similar religious crises but emerged reform Christians. Not Elizabeth. She emerged a self-assured freethinker. For the rest of her life she was repelled by organized religion, refusing to indoctrinate her children— "The memory of my own suffering has prevented me from ever shadowing one young soul with any of the superstitions of the Christian religion"—and in great age, finding herself cut loose from the now conservative woman's movement, she went after the church full force. A lifetime of listening to Bible-quoting had become emblematic for her of the divided feelings her culture sustained concerning the reality of people who are women, and in 1895 she produced the scandalous *Woman's Bible*, a piece of work that contained the feminist analysis she considered her most important.

It was in these same childhood years of lost religious faith that she also began to realize that being born a girl was seriously different from being born a boy. When Elizabeth was eleven years old, Eleazer, her only brother still alive, died. All her life she remembered going into the darkened parlor where her father sat "pale and immovable" beside the casket. She climbed up on his knee. Mechanically, he put his arms around her and then, feeling her small, strong life against his beating heart, he sighed and said, "Oh my daughter, I wish you were a boy!" In a passion of unhappiness, Elizabeth promised to become for him all that her brother had been. "All that day and far into the night," she wrote in old age, "I pondered the problem of boyhood. I thought that the chief thing to be done in order to equal boys was to be learned and courageous."

Yet the man who wished that she was a boy delighted in the animated intelligence of the girl, who seemed to experience no pleasures as great as those of reading, thinking, and talking. When her mother told her to mend her hoydenish ways, her father told her to take a walk or read a book. It was the father who loved her mind, the father who taught her to think, the father who adored her clever outbursts; and it was this same father who, later, would rebuke and nearly disown her when she acted on the independence of mind he had taught her to prize.

Sitting in her father's office, reading in his law books, listening to the endless discussion going on with either his clients or his law students—this was her favorite pastime as a child and as a girl in her teens. Everything under discussion was of interest, but the puzzle that held her attention was why women fared differently than men under the law. When she protested that the law was unjust, her father's students teased her, asking her what she intended to do about it.

One case in particular upset Elizabeth. A woman had, with her own money, bought a farm which her husband, upon his death, willed to their son. She came to lawyer Cady, who told her that there was nothing he could do for her: the law was on the husband's side. Elizabeth—then a child of perhaps ten or twelve—was shocked by her father's revelation, and thought the solution to this unfairness was to take a knife and simply cut the law out of the book lying on her father's desk. Her father gently informed her that when she grew up she might work to change the law but that this act of hers, cutting the law out of the books with a knife, was not only forbidden (it would deface the book), it was also useless. Elizabeth stared at her father. Years later, the judge might have thought back to this moment and realized that it was already too late: an educated, upright, law-and-order household had spawned a daughter who *was* going to cut the laws out of the books with a knife, not only because she found the injustice stirring, but because it excited her to feel strongly.

For a girl, feeling strongly usually meant the pursuit and consummation of romantic passion; this, from time immemorial, had been the territory over which women of temperament had squatter's rights. In Elizabeth, the parts had come together differently. Feeling strongly through sexual love was not what she would ever be about. The story has it that the romance of her young life was with her brother-in-law, Tryphena's husband, Edward Bayard, who fell in love with her and begged her to run away with him. Even if it had been possible for her to break such a powerful taboo, it is unlikely that she could have been driven to consider love her destiny. Anna Karenina yes, Emma Bovary certainly, Elizabeth Cady no. The imagination that was at work, forming her, was of an altogether other order. For Elizabeth, feeling strongly was associated—as it had been for men, also from time immemorial—not with love but with some large idea of grand doings out in the world. Deep within herself, in a place not yet made conscious, it was the world that she wanted—to be in it, and of it; to make her mark in it. And so it turned out. Her life took the outward shape of a domesticated bourgeois, but the flaring intellectual excitement that the Cause provided her, *that* was the way into her true self, and once inside that true self she was in the world. But all this lay far in the slowly articulating future.

There was no question but that the Cady girls would be educated. After all, of what use would they be as wives to ambitious men if they remained ignorant of social graces, and without the developed good sense that a reasonable amount of book learning could instill? As children they attended the local academy for girls, and at fifteen were sent to Emma Willard's Female Seminary in Troy, New York. Willard was a well-known progressive educator who wanted to provide middle-class girls with the equivalent of a college education, and in 1830 it was considered that she did. For three years, Elizabeth was tutored in philosophy, logic, rhetoric, and the sciences—at home, she also studied Greek with a neighborly minister—and emerged as educated a young woman as any in her class, and far better able to think than most. Then at eighteen it was over. Suddenly, she was back home for good. Now what was she supposed to do? Well . . . nothing, really. Sit down and wait for marriage. Restlessness of a high, stubborn order set in: no one appealed, and no one was *likely* to appeal. In hardly any time at all she was in danger of becoming a spinster.

She had gone often to the home, also in upstate New York, of her cousin Gerrit Smith, and now, as a young woman at loose ends, she became (not entirely with her parents' consent) a constant visitor there. Gerrit Smith was a rich radical, a passionate (and in his time famous) abolitionist of expansive personality and great hospitality who loved inviting the world into his home; his house was also a stop on the Underground Railroad. The people who sat down at Smith's table bore little resemblance to those at her father's. Here, the talk was alive with liberal and unguarded opinion. It was at Gerrit's that she discovered she had a craving for conversational boldness.

The talk was of slavery. From the first that she heard it, she knew this talk was important: it touched on a set of ideas wholly different from those stressed in her own home, where all talk of politics and society was rooted in one's knee-jerk obligation to God, rather than in the open question of what man's obligation is to man, and to what lengths one was willing or able to go in the name of *this* obligation. At Gerrit Smith's the distance was pretty far. Abolition stirred Elizabeth's soul certainly because she found slavery appalling, but mainly because it fired these men and women whose sensibilities thrilled her.

Abolitionism was something distinct from the commonplace objection to slavery. In the America of the 1830s and '40s, a very large part of the population—including Elizabeth's parents—was anti-slavery, but not immoderately so. The ordinary person who opposed slavery, whether on religious grounds or out of liberal sentiment, urged a course of action that would peacefully encourage the practice to slowly die out. At the same time, many anti-slavers did not look forward to absorbing freed blacks into American life (Harriet Beecher Stowe, typically, has her runaway slaves shipping out for Africa at the end of *Uncle Tom's Cabin*). These people were appalled by the *idea* of slavery, but they did not look upon the end of slavery as an opportunity to extend their thoughts to the question of universal rights. For them, abolitionists were the radical left: frightening extremists, potential terrorists, a possible cause of civil war (think IRA, think Israel's Irgun, or Castro's guerilla fighters). Although abolitionists themselves were split between those who shared the moral fervor of a William Lloyd Garrison (who was indeed willing to risk war: "No union with slaveholders!") and those who hoped to force political change without bloodshed, to the uninformed the abolitionists were all one. For the young Elizabeth Cady, listening to the arguments at Smith's table, night after month after year, sitting next to her closest intimate, Gerrit's daughter Libby, the differences were also negligible. The ardor of abolitionists was thrilling. The more moral fervor the better, but any abolitionist was better than no abolitionist. For her, only they had politics—and politics, she was beginning to see, was what stirred her right down to the center.

It was at Smith's home, in 1839, when she was twenty-four, that she met Henry Stanton, ten years older and already a well-known abolitionist speaker and organizer, as well as an officer in the New York State Anti-Slavery Society. She was everything that a man like Stanton could want: so smart, so responsive, and just sufficiently adoring of his political celebrity. Henry was absolutely delighted. He pursued her, and he won her. A month after they met, on another visit to her cousin's, she engaged herself to him and then went home to announce her newly accomplished destiny. A storm of parental protest engulfed her. An abolitionist? A professional radical? A man with no real means of support? Lizzie, are you kidding?

She was dumbfounded and told Henry that she did not know what on earth to do. There then began, between the two men, her father and her lover, a struggle to obtain her loyalty and control her future. Judge Cady tormented his enamored daughter. Henry badgered his beleaguered sweetheart. Between the two of them, she felt herself being torn apart. "These two noble men," she wrote later, "who would have done anything for my happiness . . . turned the sweetest dream of my life into a tragedy. How little strong men, with their logic, sophistry, and hypothetical examples, appreciate the violence they inflict on a woman's heart, in trying to subjugate her to their will! The love of protecting too often degenerates into downright tyranny."

Elizabeth broke the engagement, and sat down to pine for a lost life. Then, in the early part of 1840, Henry held out the carrot she could not help reaching for. He had been invited to come as a delegate to the World Anti-Slavery Convention due to be held in London in June of that year. If they were husband and wife she could come with him. *This* she could not bear to pass up. For this, she was willing to risk all. In May, half expecting to be disowned by her father, she married Henry, insisting—to her husband's acquiescent amusement—on keeping her maiden name as well as taking on his. Off she sailed for England under the name she would eventually make famous. The trip was an exciting prefiguration of much that was to come. Many people who met them, both on the ship and later in London, remembered the couple well: wonderful little Mrs. Stanton, so refreshingly outspoken in her views and so unpretentious in her manner—and Mr. Stanton, somewhat too aware of himself, and remarkably, even pompously, overbearing toward *her*. How quickly he had emerged a husband, how heedlessly she was becoming a wife.

Upon her arrival at the convention, the most extraordinary thing happened to Elizabeth Cady Stanton: the people in charge refused to seat her. Not only her, but all who looked like her; that is, women. Elizabeth was amazed. A meeting called in the name of equality for all would not seat members of the female sex. Not a single woman who had come to London to attend the convention—and from America there were many—would be permitted to speak. All were required to retire to a peripheral place in the convention hall where they could see but not be seen, hear but not be heard.

Henry Stanton was disturbed, but not that disturbed: he took his place in the hall. William Lloyd Garrison, on the other hand, would not. The great zealot had crossed an ocean to appear at this convention—all within were waiting for the words of the famous American—but Garrison's politics ran deep and true. He meant it when he said equality for all. If the women couldn't speak, neither would he. Lucretia Mott—patient, intelligent, twenty years older, also not seated at the conference—walked Elizabeth around London, and explained the reality of the larger world in which she lived, the one that she had until now not actually experienced. Elizabeth was twenty-five years old. With all the thinking she had done about slavery, liberty, and the American idea, it had never dawned on her until this moment: when the democracy was conceived, *she* was not what was had in mind.

She never got over that flash of plain sight. It was her moment of conversion—the moment when she realized that "in the eyes of the world I was not as I was in my own eyes, I was only a woman." In her writing we see the memory of London, 1840, return repeatedly to make her burn anew.

Twelve years later, in 1852, she wrote to Susan B. Anthony:

I have been re-reading the report of [the 1840 convention]. How thoroughly humiliating it was to us! How I could have sat there quietly and listened to all that was said and done, I do not now understand . . . In the good time coming, what a cause of wonder it will be to recall the fact that the champions of freedom, the most progressive men of the 19th century, denied women the right of free speech in an anti-slavery convention, when, at the same time, they would have received with éclat the most degraded man from a rice plantation. If Sambo [an epithet she used when in a rage] had been cast out of the convention for any reason, I wonder if Wendell Phillips and George Thompson [American abolitionists at the convention] would have coolly remarked on his discomfiture, "Well, he is as happy outside as in!" Men and angels, give me patience. I am at the boiling point.

And eighteen years later, in 1858, at the Eighth National Woman's Rights Convention, she recalls what returning home from London in 1840 had meant:

That last meeting of the American Anti-Slavery Society, in New York City [before the women left to form their own organization], ought to be familiar to the mind of every woman in our movement. In no public assembly on record did the ridiculous ever reach such a climax of absurdity. There were clergymen urging women to vote on the question whether, henceforth, women should be permitted to vote in that organization—calling on them to do there, what they declared it a sin for them to do anywhere. It was a stormy meeting, held that day, by the friends of the slave. And though he still groaned in his Southern house of bondage, they decided that woman's voice should not be heard on his behalf.

While children set for middle-class respectability often exhibit an early talent for art or science or intellection, it is impossible to predict accurately the one in whom the giftedness will blossom not into a pastime, but into a driving need: the kind of need that determines the whole of one's future life. Radicalism, too, is a talent that proves formative rather than casual. In creative work, the driving need occurs when the talent is exercised, the possessor of it finds that she or he is struck to the heart (not a thing that happens simply because one has talent), and a sense of expressive existence flares into bright life. That experience is incomparable: to feel not simply alive, but expressive. It induces a conviction of inner clarity that quickly becomes the very thing one can no longer do without. If it *can* be done without, it usually is. Those destined for a life of professional

27

radicalism experience themselves in exactly the same way as does the artist or scientist who reaches center through the practice of the gift. No reward of life—not love or fame or wealth—can compete. It is to this clarity of inner being that the radical—like the artist, the scientist, the philosopher—becomes attached, even addicted.

This, I think, is what happened to Elizabeth Stanton in London when the anti-slavery conference refused to seat her. She had embraced the cause of abolition—not merely anti-slavery, but *abolition*—because the passion of men like Gerrit Smith and Henry Stanton had aroused her capacity for strong response. But when *they*, these good and great people whom she had held up as paragons among men, told her now, in 1840, both in London and in New York, that she couldn't speak, she could only sit and listen, the power of radical fire was ignited in her, and she understood herself in a way that she had not before. *This* was the cause that clarified her—the one that told her, not approximately but precisely, who she was—the one that, within ten years, would become the thing she could no longer do without.

II

1848

A RADICAL AMONG RADICALS

T RUE, THE FIRE TOOK EIGHT YEARS to flare into an open blaze. Elizabeth and Henry had come home in 1841 to her father's house, where the Cadys struggled to accept a son-in-law they would never love. Here, the couple settled in for an indefinite while, and Henry—both to ingratiate himself and to learn a trade—studied law with Judge Cady. When he felt sufficiently schooled to complete his education elsewhere, he proposed to Elizabeth—who readily agreed—that they live in Boston. Before they left upstate New York, she received a letter from Angelina Grimké, whom she had met through Henry, urging her not to make this move.

"There is much, very much there [in Boston], to gratify the taste and the intellect," Angelina wrote,

> and thou wilt greatly enjoy the high mental improvement which exists there . . . But too often they take the place of better things and leave the heart unpenetrated by the love of God, uninfluenced by the love of our fellow creatures . . . I greatly fear this contact for thee, because

thou has not given thy heart to God, and therefore this preserving power cannot uphold thee. He has blessed thee with talents which if devoted to his service will be a blessing to thy self, to thy husband and family, and to the world . . . In Boston there will be little to make thee so, much to draw your heart away from God. I long to see you sitting at the feet of Jesus, hearing his words and doing his will. This is all you need to place you among the choicest instruments for doing good.

The Grimké sisters (Sarah and Angelina) were passionately religious workers in the cause of both anti-slavery and women's rights; Angelina was, as well, an inspired preacher. Her letter is a perfect demonstration of nineteenth-century religious thought and feeling interwoven with social reform. In abolitionism, especially, the missionary sense of doing God's work was powerful: deep, ardent, narrow. Giving one's heart to God was a euphemism for taking seriously, within the scope of Christian dictates, the corrective work of an unredeemed world. Every reform movement of the early nineteenth century was riddled with this language. Angelina Grimké cannot imagine a centered human being, one who is meant to perform significantly, cohering unless these sentences are guiding her. A godless encounter with the world that will prove useful is unthinkable. Without the stabilizing force of "coming to Jesus," it is inevitable that Elizabeth will fragment: lose or corrupt the considerable gifts of mind and spirit that Angelina knows her to possess.

Of all the passions for reform that would lead nineteenth-century minds inexorably out of the rich dark rhetoric of Christian devotion into the glaring skepticism of secular insight, certainly women's rights was among the foremost; and of all the feminists whose rhetoric would, in time, reflect the immensity of this shift in shared sensibility none is bolder than Elizabeth Stanton. It is not easy to explain how it was that sentences free of religious restraint began to compel her consciousness, but once she had her first *full* free thought, she became Alice falling down the rabbit-hole into the upside-down world where hard truth alone is spoken, a world from which there is no return. I've often wondered what Elizabeth actually thought, twenty-five years old, reading that letter in her father's house in 1842, with her husband waiting in the doorway to take her out into the married life that would ultimately lead her to a vocabulary and a sentence structure that Angelina Grimké might well have considered a ticket to perdition.

In Boston, through abolitionist friends, the Stantons met "everyone" and went "everywhere" and, unexpectedly, Elizabeth came to glory in the open sprawl of city life while Henry languished. It was here in Boston that each of them might have begun to see the qualities in themselves that ultimately proved them incompatible; it was to be years, however, before the information now being made available to them would register consciously.

Elizabeth delighted in motherhood and homemaking; it was her first real job, and it pleased her to be good at it. At the same time, she also read, went to meetings, joined conversation clubs, attended lectures, and entertained; the list of people at her dinner table in Boston reads like a who's who of nineteenth-century reform: Lydia Child, Parker Pillsbury, Frederick Douglass, Maria Weston Chapman, John Greenleaf Whittier, Theodore Parker, Bronson Alcott—as well as Emerson, James Russell Lowell, and Hawthorne. There was not a time in her life when she was not responding to whatever largeness was available. Everything Elizabeth saw, heard, and did in the big city was of intense interest, including a visit to Brook Farm where she admired the Transcendentalist experiment in communal living.

For Henry, it was distinctly otherwise. Henry Stanton hungered for public office and, starting here and now, in Boston in the early forties, a lifelong pattern regarding this hunger began to emerge. He came to be known as a man for whom political success was more urgent than principles, and somehow, this worked repeatedly against him. He would seek office, come close to achieving it, and in the end it would elude him. He could never pull it together; could not induce the necessary trust and interest in the machine politicians who, at any given moment, held the keys to the kingdom. He ran here, he ran there. He switched parties and platforms. He told this segment of a political party, Yes! Yes! Yes! He told that one, Yes! Yes! Yes! And when all was said and done, he was not the one chosen. A lifetime of low-level hope and humiliation wore away at him; and bit by bit, drained off Elizabeth's respect. She, for whom principle remained everything, found herself bound for life to a once-idealistic man for whom expedience slowly became all.

Within a few short years in Boston, Henry began to experience the pain of his first political failure. Garrisonian abolitionists, of whom he was not one, dominated the town, making it impossible for him to feel effective. "I hope the sad divisions in the anti-slavery cause will not deprive you of the pleasure of being acquainted with the noble women who are on the other side," Angelina Grimké had written to Elizabeth—and for Elizabeth, who *was* a Garrisonian, the divisions did not signify. But Henry needed to feel central to his immediate surroundings; if not, he suffered. Unable to make his mark in the larger sphere, he would rather retire to a smaller one where he *could* signify. Besides, he said, his lungs were being compromised by the damp air of Boston.

It was decided that they would leave the city for the country—for the sake of Henry's lungs, Elizabeth wrote her friends—and they soon moved to the village of Seneca Falls in upstate New York (just far enough from the Cady home) into a house that Elizabeth's father bought for them. Here, Henry's life settled into a combination of unsuccessful bids for political office and a fairly successful second career as a political journalist, both pursuits taking him regularly and repeatedly from home, to Albany and Washington. Elizabeth, meanwhile, lived the significant portion of her married-mothering life to the full in this little village: she stayed home, encouraged her man, got repeatedly pregnant—and wrote letters. In time, she came to burn over the arrangement. It was not so much that she wanted Henry home. She envied his freedom. "How rebellious it makes me feel," she was writing within ten years, "when I see Henry going about where and how he pleases. He can walk at will through the whole wide world or shut himself up alone . . . [while] I have been compelled to hold all my noblest aspirations in abeyance in order to be a wife, a mother, a nurse, a cook, a household drudge."

After London, Stanton was never again without feminist connection. Her correspondence was extraordinarily inclusive and lively, especially in her contact with Lucretia Mott; Lucretia's sister, Martha Wright, who lived not far from Seneca Falls; and the Grimké sisters. Lucretia Mott and Angelina Grimké were waging a struggle within their own religious movements—the Quaker and the Congregationalist—for the right of women to talk in public on behalf of abolition, as in those movements, too, the men beside whom they worked equally for the Great Cause could not feel the justice in a woman's need to speak her mind *out loud*. Somewhere, just below the level of gathered thought, Stanton was taking important notes on the progress of this debate, at the same time that the profound isolation of total domesticity was beginning to eat into her.

Absorbed as she was by every new piece of experience that came her way—her capacity for animated interest, witty conversation, fun and entertainment, uncommon among the famous feminists of her generation—for the first years of marriage she was fully taken up by the business of making a home and having babies. A supremely healthy animal by her own account—and in this she gloried—she gave birth like a peasant in the field: labor would begin; she'd push out the baby, clean herself up, and be up and about in twenty-four hours. In the end, she had seven of them, and she was most tender-hearted toward the little creatures who had come out of her body. Raising them up to be human beings set her a problem that she embraced wholeheartedly; but when they were grown the children became people, most of whom did not hold her real interest. While her affections remained strong they grew absentminded, and she looked back on motherhood as a full-time occupation with distinctly mixed feelings. "I now fully understood," she wrote years later, "the practical difficulties most women had to contend with in the isolated household and the impossibility of woman's development if in contact, the chief part of her life, with servants and children."

Among intelligent American women of her class the conversation about women's lives had, in a sense, been going on all around her for years, and at almost every level of intellectual engagement, ranging in tone and depth from the high-minded to the respectably minded: that is, from Margaret Fuller to *Little Women*. Essentially, this conversation turned on an argument for education for women that was made on behalf of the General Good—namely, that an educated wife and mother would know better how to influence men and boys toward enlightened citizenship. In Fuller's circle the question might be framed in Emersonian considerations of the "true" meaning and value of reliance upon the self. In temperance circles, the weight came down on Christian virtue. Among those who had no taste for either activism or philosophy, the price of idealism was to be weighed rather than agreed upon. One can easily imagine a conversation among the March sisters after they've come across *The Vindication of the Rights of Woman*:

"She's absolutely right, and I say bully for her!" cries Jo in 1860, tossing her hat in the air. "I intend to fight for women's rights. Won't it be fun, Bethy, stomping around New York with an Education for Women placard on my chest?"

"Oh Jo!" breathes Beth, eyes shining feverishly, "you *are* the bravest soul in the world."

"Josephine," says Meg primly. "Pick up your hat, and speak sensibly. If all husbands were as good as my John there'd be no need for women's rights."

"But all men *aren't* as good as your John," replies Amy tartly. "Nevertheless, Jo won't be so brave when she is called un-natural, and is deprived of respectable society, as anyone involved with women's rights is bound to be."

Between Margaret Fuller and Louisa May Alcott stands the considerably more complicated example of Lydia Maria Child, a writer of talent and intelligence who, for money, wrote popular books for women gathered under the rubric *The Ladies' Family Library*, while she lent her real brains to the anti-slavery cause. Married to a Garrisonian abolitionist, and she herself passionate for the cause, Lydia Child was distinctly relieved to turn from the risk-taking pressures of abolition to what she thought of as the simplicity of the conventions surrounding women's lives.

In 1833, Child (the first woman to be allowed reading privileges in the Boston Athenaeum) wrote a powerful piece of radicalism called *An Appeal in Favor of That Class of Americans Called Africans*, which froze her out of middle-class approval of moderate opinion (her Athenaeum privileges were revoked). Unhappy over this development

in her life—Child, like Amy March, had need of respectable society—
she thought to cheer herself up by writing a history of "true wom-
anhood" (a phrase that crops up repeatedly in the mid–nineteenth
century); but she came across a wealth of information testifying to
an immense variety among the women rising up out of history and,
two years later, in 1835, published *History of the Condition of Women, in
Various Ages and Nations*, a book that a coming generation of feminists
would turn to as a major reference. Child herself, however, remained
only a fellow traveler of the women's movement, quoting Byron, who
said, "I care not how blue a woman's stockings are if her skirts are
long enough to cover them."

The inner life of the women of Stanton's class was saturated in
the rhetoric of Christian obligation, and psychologically hemmed in
by a penetrating belief in woman's natural identity as wife and
mother. To break free of such deeply internalized concepts was not
only no easy task, it was almost impossible to find the sentences that
would allow a woman to frame the thoughts that would help her step
away from the welcome activism of piecemeal reform into a philosophically inclusive view of the way that the life of a person who is
a woman is formed and shaped by the culture. With all the reforms
continually being urged—most having to do with legislation that
would allow married women to retain the legal rights that had been
theirs before marriage—it was almost never suggested that the overriding conviction that life is divided into separate spheres, a woman's
sphere of action and a man's, is false and needed to be abolished.

Yet the 1830s and '40s in America was a time of astonishing
public spiritedness, made up equally of cocky self-belief and raging
self-criticism. Americans still felt giddy over the success of the
Revolution, and wonderfully reinforced by a surge of influence coming from abroad—all that democratic uprising, all that German

Romanticism—the influence upon which Emerson was building a life's work of belief in individuation; but there was slavery, undreamt-of capitalist rapacity, and the despair of working-class alcoholism. So, looking one way at American life you had Transcendentalism and the thrilling promise of "self-union"; looking another, you had a mounting fury over broken republican promises and a pressing call for abolition, temperance, and universal education. Either way, the internal stir in the country was acutely *felt*, and somewhere in the shared sensibility, the feeling combined with an emotional conviction that the American democracy was intimately tied to a God-given right that every American would engage with life in the immediate surround. If your imagination was stirred by the promise of spiritual liberation, you were drawn to Transcendentalism; if it yearned for republican democracy, you joined the ranks of Reform—very much as in our own time, during the 1960s, the irresistible stir of a soaring activist spirit prompted one either toward the counterculture or into the New Left. And again, as in our own time, it seems inevitable in hindsight that, given such an atmosphere, there would be another uprising of the women. For Stanton, it began with her contested right, from within the Left of her time, to take an intellectually active part in the Great Cause. One hundred and twenty-five years later, when my generation of feminists emerged from within the ranks of the New Left opposing the Vietnam War, the circumstance was cruder—a woman in SDS got up at a meeting to complain of sexism in the organization, and the men in the audience hooted, "Take her off the stage and fuck her!"—but the impact, and the consequence, was the same.

Out of the ranks of the abolitionist movement came every important radical feminist of the nineteenth century—just as before them, in England, Wollstonecraft had emerged out of radical support for the French Revolution, and forty years after her, again in England, Frances Wright had come out of Owenite socialism. In all cases, the experience of the organized Left was key. Invariably, "the movement" did for the women what, until then, they could not do for themselves: it educated them to political work, made organizers of them, taught them how to frame an argument, debate the question, and hold an audience. Then, after it had educated them, it clarified them: made them see clearly where *they* stood, in the eyes of their comrades, on the large landscape of universal human rights.

For Stanton, the education, ultimately, would be worth its weight in gold. On the one hand, it taught her that Garrisonian moral suasion was, for her, *the* instrument of political reform. "By the foolishness of preaching," she once wrote, "must all moral revolutions be achieved." This approach alone, she concluded, would keep a reformer honest, and encourage a principled independence of mind unlikely to be seduced by expediency. On the other hand, she saw, too, that women's rights, in every radical movement ever launched, had commanded only secondary interest and respect. Slavery and freedom? Yes! Capital and labor? Definitely! Enfranchisement for women? Of course, of course, but . . . not just now. How many times over the next forty years must she have experienced that hot, hard amazement that every woman feels when forced to realize that in the cause of women's rights men do not see the cause of humanity itself at stake; *never* would it seem an urgency to any but the women themselves. Women's rights, Stanton would at last realize, was permanently on its own. Women must work—alone and for themselves—and the trick would be to let nothing subvert the singlemindedness of their necessity.

As they sat around a tea table in Waterloo (a village not far from Seneca Falls) in July of 1848, Stanton and her friends—the visiting

Lucretia Mott, Martha Wright, and their mutual friend Mary Ann McClintock—got so exercised discussing the current New York State debate over whether to allow married women to hold title to their own property (the debate itself had long infuriated Stanton) that they decided then and there to finally hold a meeting to discuss women's rights, and "before twilight deepened into night, the call was written." On July 11, the *Seneca County Courier* published a notice advising that a "convention to discuss the social, civil, and religious condition and rights of woman" was scheduled to open only five days later, on July 19. "Rain or shine," Stanton wrote on July 14 to her friends in Waterloo,

> I intend to spend Sunday with you that we may all together concoct a declaration. I have drawn up one but you may suggest any alterations & improvements for I know it is not as perfect a declaration as should go forth from the first woman's rights convention that has ever assembled. I shall take the ten o'clock train in the morning & return at five in the evening, provided we can accomplish *all our business* in that time. I have written to Lydia Maria Child, Maria Chapman & Sarah Grimké, as we hope for some good letters to read in the convention.

It was in the course of drafting the *Declaration of Sentiments*—the document of complaint that she put together for the Seneca Falls convention—that Stanton stumbled on her own inclination to frame the situation, and the argument, in radical largeness. What she had "drawn up" was a set of resolutions that had taken shape in her head out of the inspired notion of using the Declaration of Independence as a model for complaint. Simply by adding "and woman" all the way through—"We hold these truths to be self-evident, that all men and women"—Stanton's organizing principle had been set in place.

She was able, then, to introduce her subject by drawing way back from the limited immediacy of women-and-property, or women-and-education, or women-and-custody, beginning with the observation that the eighteenth-century English jurist William Blackstone had made in his influential work *Commentaries on the Laws of England*, when he pointed out that it is in the very nature of things that man's deepest need is to "pursue his own true and substantial happiness," and further that, as this is a law of nature dictated by God himself, it is only right that all other laws be required to honor it. Thus, Stanton's declaration concluded, this convention would be resolved that "such laws as conflict, in any way, with the true and substantial happiness of woman, are contrary to the great precept of nature, and of no validity." For this is a concept that, as Blackstone himself had said, carries all before it, and therefore it only followed that "all laws which prevent woman from occupying such a station in society as her conscience shall dictate or which place her in a position inferior to that of man, are contrary to the great precept of nature, and therefore of no force or authority."

The world in which American women actually live, she went on, was a far cry from the one dictated by Blackstone's eloquent first-principle-of-life; it was, in fact, an *affront* to the principle; and the women of this country never sounded more ignorant than when asserting that they have all the rights they want. A double standard prevailed throughout our shared social existence, one in which women were denied the right to free and open intellectual inquiry; punished for what men do with impunity; confined within a circumscribed limit of action that corrupt customs and a perverted application of the scriptures had marked out for them; and denied the sacred right—that was her word, "sacred"—to the elective franchise. In

short, women lived perpetually unfitted for participation in the public enterprise that engaged the entire human race.

She had written fully, freely, and directly, without tact or political caution, engrossed only by where the argument was going, where
uncensored thought would lead her. Henry, leaning over her shoulder, drew back startled. "You ask for suffrage," he said, "and I'm
leaving town." (He did.) Lucretia Mott put her hand over her mouth.
"O Lizzie, thou wilt make us ridiculous." But neither of them could
make a dent in her.

How *fast* her mind had gone to work once she had something serious to think about. Throughout the 1840s, her letters are filled
with chitchat and gossip—she and Henry are undecided as to what
they'll do or where they'll live; they're going to Peterboro in the
morning; cousin Gerrit is making a match between Mr. Birney and
Nancy's sister, Elizabeth Fitzhugh; she spent two weeks in New York
but didn't see Angelina Grimké as she was "on the eve of confine-
ment"; how *do* you make that delicious dessert—but in 1849, within
less than a year after the Seneca Falls convention, she is writing
briskly to Mary Anne Johnson, an early feminist comrade:

> Dear Mary Anne, How rejoiced I am to hear that the
> women of Ohio have called a Convention preparatory to
> the remodeling of their State Constitution . . . It is
> important now that a change is proposed that [women]
> speak, and loudly too. Having decided to petition for a
> redress of grievances, the question is *for what shall you first*
> *petition?* For the exercise of your right to the elective
> franchise—nothing short of this. The grant to you of this
> right will secure all others, and the granting of every other

right, whilst this is denied, is a mockery. For instance:
What is the right to property, without the right to protect
it? The enjoyment of that right today is no security that it
will be continued tomorrow, so long as it is granted to us
as a favor, and not claimed by us as a right . . . Depend
upon it, this is the point to attack the stronghold of the
fortress—*the one* woman will find most difficult to take—
the one man will most reluctantly give up.

And *this* letter went on for forty years.

Once the idea of suffrage had occurred, and she'd seen it in all
its dazzling rightness, nothing and no one could make her back
down. Yes, family was delicious, and politics exciting, but now that
she was thinking she felt brave, generous, unequivocal; alive and
whole. To go forward *into* her thought was her only compulsion.
Women's rights—then as always—was the catalyst, but it was life on
the intellectual barricades that supplied the chemical attraction. *This*
was where she now lived. Only the love of thinking could harness the
resentment over inequality; in the early years it gave her the energy to
care for five, six, seven children during the day and sit down at midnight at the kitchen table to write a two-hour speech that demanded
to know what it means to be a human being. This passion for thought
brought her finally to a definition of independence that would speak
intimately to millions of women alive more than a century later, even
though it spoke to only a fraction of those alive in her own time.

On the second day of the 1848 convention Stanton's resolutions
were formally adopted. Framed in her famous play on Jeffersonian
language—"We hold these truths to be self-evident: that all men and
women are created equal . . . [although] the history of mankind is a

history of repeated injuries and usurpations on the part of man toward woman"—the full indictment runs as follows:

He has never permitted her to exercise her inalienable right to the elective franchise.

He has compelled her to submit to laws, in the formation of which she had no voice.

He has withheld from her rights which are given to the most ignorant and degraded men—both natives and foreigners.

He has made her, if married, in the eyes of the law, civilly dead.

He has made her, morally, an irresponsible being, as she can commit crimes with impunity, provided they be done in the presence of her husband.

In the covenant of marriage, she is compelled to promise obedience to her husband, he becoming, to all intents and purposes, her master—the law giving him power to deprive her of her liberty, and to administer chastisement.

He has so framed the laws of divorce [that he decides on] what shall be the proper causes of divorce; and in case of separation, to whom the guardianship of the children shall be given; the law in all cases giving all power into his hands.

After depriving her of all rights as a married woman, if single and the owner of property, he has taxed her to support a government which recognizes her only when her property can be made profitable to it.

He has denied her a thorough education—all colleges being closed to her.

He allows her in Church as well as State but a subordinate position, claiming apostolic authority for her exclusion from the ministry.

He has created a false public sentiment, by giving to the world a

different code of morals for men and women, by which moral delin-
quencies that exclude women from society are not only tolerated but
deemed of little account in man.

He has usurped the prerogative of Jehovah himself, claiming it as
his right to assign for her a sphere of action, when that belongs to her
conscience and her God.

He has endeavored in every way that he could to destroy her con-
fidence in her own powers, to lessen her self-respect, and to make her
willing to lead a dependent and abject life.

Now, in view of this entire disfranchisement of one-half the
people of this country, their social and religious degradation—in view
of the unjust laws above mentioned, and because women do feel themselves aggrieved, oppressed, and fraudulently deprived of their most
sacred rights, we insist that they have immediate admission to all the
rights and privileges which belong to them as citizens of these United
States.

A hundred people signed this document: seventy women and
thirty men, among the men, Frederick Douglass. It is significant that
later many of the signatories un-signed themselves—as, in a sense,
they would go on doing for the next 150 years—but on that July
afternoon in 1848 in Seneca Falls Elizabeth Stanton's powers of
persuasion prevailed over the ever-recurring anxieties that women's
rights would inevitably arouse. The situation had been laid out so
thoroughly and so lucidly that nearly every person in the room could
endorse without difficulty each resolution as it was put forward. The
only radical demand was the one made for the vote. That scared almost everyone in the room ("Lizzie, thou wilt make us ridiculous"),
and the resolution was barely carried by a majority vote of two. Yet
no sooner had Stanton framed the demand than everyone saw what

she saw: that this was the right, as she was to repeat times without number, by which all others would be secured, the one without which all others would come to little or nothing. Without suffrage, she had suddenly understood, one was not a citizen. Without citizenship, the Rights of Man did not apply. Not to *you*, at any rate, who, beyond the pale of political definition, did not, in the eyes of the law, exist. All this she saw simply because in mid-July of 1848 she had looked at the American Declaration of Independence—"looked and saw"—with the kind of newly charged interest that transforms a complaint into an imperative.

The Seneca Falls convention was widely reported on, and it met with a ridicule that had been anticipated. Yet, when it came, Stanton experienced it as a shock to the nervous system. The *Declaration of Sentiments* was described in the newspapers as a parody of a sacred document, and at home, in Seneca Falls itself, a sermon was preached the Sunday after the newspaper report, with the preacher thundering "Infidel!" at the feminists. Taken aback, Stanton retorted hotly, "When no conclusive arguments can be brought to bear upon a subject a cry of 'infidelity' is [always] raised ... No reform has ever been started but that the Bible, falsely interpreted, has opposed it ... It seems to us, the time has fully come for this much abused book to change hands."

She had been certain that all reasonable, right-thinking persons would quickly see what she saw, and begin the (granted) arduous task of righting the matter of woman's grievance before the law—not only for the sake of simple justice, but for that of the Rights of Man and the welfare of the republic. It was hard to believe that serious opposition was going to be seriously mounted against the cause of women's rights. Within the year, however, she had begun to understand otherwise. She was made to see the depth of unreality that a person who is a woman embodied not only for those in power, but for the mass of people living lives of ordinary appetite and acquisition, shrouded in received wisdoms so long unreviewed that they seemed at one with nature. This, Stanton saw, was what women's rights was up against; not the strength of cynical political opposition, but the far greater strength of a cultural innocence that, like an animal in its lair, remains benign if ignored but becomes dangerous when prodded. She saw this because her own father announced himself an enemy.

Daniel Cady: jurist, statesman, defender of the republic and upright Calvinist. Until the day he died, he hated every word on women's rights that came out of Elizabeth's mouth. It was her father who made her understand the strength of blind cultural belief: what it would mean for the ordinary woman to take so radical a step as announcing herself a feminist. "To think," she wrote bitterly to Susan Anthony in 1852, "that all in me of which my father would have felt a proper pride had I been a man, is deeply mortifying to him because I am a woman . . . I never felt more keenly the degradation of my sex." But, as she also wrote, the iron had entered into her soul. She was a grown-up woman now, fully formed, and undivided within herself. When the cause of women's rights clarified her, it induced in her a wholeness of being to which, for the rest of her life, she owed primary loyalty.

Her temperament was extreme; simple actually, but extreme. To all who ever knew her, the self-confidence was extraordinary. She might have taken Flaubert's dictum, "Dress like a bourgeois, think like a revolutionary" for her motto. She observed the social amenities—good manners and proper dress—but nothing could make her moderate her thought. She hardly ever spoke before she thought, but she always spoke without consultation or strategic consideration. Her intellectual independence was experienced by many as high-handedness: it broke party ranks, alienated radicals and reformers alike, and, in time, drove away countless others whose good will she could have used. But what she needed—vain and imperious as she was—was to speak truth as she saw it at any given moment. That is what she *needed*. She needed it more than she needed the approval of family or steady comradeship or even political success. The need often made her reckless, hot-tempered, and insensitive.

In her memoir she tells of how after she had written her obituary of Lucretia Mott, she received a letter from a man who accused her of using an anecdote of his without attribution. "I laughed him to scorn," she writes, "that he should have thought it was my duty to have done so. I told him plainly that he belonged to a class of citizens who had robbed me of all civil and political rights . . . and now it ill became him to call me to account for using one of his little anecdotes that, ten to one, he had cribbed from some woman . . . I told him that he should feel highly complimented, instead of complaining, that he had written something I thought worth using."

In Nebraska in 1875, out on the circuit, she is baited by a man in the audience. "My wife has presented me with eight beautiful children," he announces. "Is not this a better life work than that of exercising the right of suffrage?" Stanton looks him up and down and says, "I have met few men worth repeating eight times."

On a Sunday afternoon—also in the 1870s—sitting in a railroad hotel, she writes to her daughter Margaret—who has written to ask if it is not lonely traveling as she does—"It is indeed, and I should have enjoyed above all things having Hattie with me." Sensitive mother! Hattie is Margaret's sister, Harriot, Stanton's favorite child.

In 1872 all New York was buzzing with the Beecher-Tilton

scandal. Henry Ward Beecher, the most famous minister in the country, was on trial for committing adultery with Elizabeth Tilton, a married parishioner. Susan Anthony, the soul of rectitude who knew the principals intimately, would speak not a word on the subject. Stanton, on the other hand, ran around town, both talking and writing freely on the case—advocating divorce in hot, sweeping terms, thereby prompting a suffragist in Chicago to write in the *Tribune*, "Of course, Mrs. Stanton has a right to her opinions, but I question her prerogative to load the Woman Suffrage Movement with their dead weight."

She had a sharp tongue—ironic, mocking, challenging. Writing scornfully of upper-class women who opposed suffrage, she says,

> Who that has mingled with this class, is ignorant of the senseless round, the utter vacuity of such an existence. The woman who has no fixed purpose in her life is like a traveler at the depot, waiting hour after hour for the cars to come in—listless, uneasy, expectant—with this difference, the traveler has a definite object to look for, whereas the woman is simply waiting for something to "turn up" . . . She may write books, but they are popular only so far as they echo back man's thunder, hence our literary women instead of dealing stout blows . . . are all trimming their sails to the popular breeze . . . Had [they] "all the rights they want," we should have better books from them on subjects which they understand and feel most deeply.

As time went by, she got more and more on people's nerves, but she experienced her own radicalism as political destiny:

> The history of the world shows that the vast majority, in every generation, passively accept the conditions into which they are born, while

those who demand larger liberties are ever a small, ostracized minority, whose claims are ridiculed and ignored . . . That a majority of the women of the United States accept, without protest, the disabilities which grow out of their disenfranchisement is simply an evidence of their ignorance and cowardice, while the minority who demand a higher political status clearly prove their superior intelligence and wisdom.

It galled her—as it has many others before and after her—that the majority of women in her country did not see clearly on the matter of their own rights, and this grievance held her attention year after year after year.

In 1848 at Seneca Falls, she wrote, "Resolved, that the women of this country ought to be enlightened in regard to the laws under which they live, that they may no longer publish their degradation, by declaring themselves satisfied with their present position, nor their ignorance, by asserting that they have all the rights they want."

Twenty years later, as she sat alone, with the full meaning of suffrage repeatedly looming up before her, she was still filled with angry wonder "at the apathy and indifference of our women" to the necessity of the vote.

The resistance to suffrage brought out the worst in her as well as the best. Half a century in service to The Cause made Stanton both wise and astonishingly intemperate. When at peace with herself— that is, hopeful—she spoke like a philosopher; when demoralized, a racist and an elitist. Like Virginia Woolf sitting in the British Museum fifty years later, looking at the clerk with the spotted tie, Stanton also could not believe that the great unwashed—that is, blacks, immigrants, the uneducated—were going to walk through the door of suffrage just because they were men, while she who was rich, intelligent, and native born would still be standing on the other side, begging.

When she was asked why women wanted the vote—after all, were they not already adequately represented by their fathers, husbands, and brothers?—she would invariably reply, Let the law books answer that question. Take a look at the laws, she said, and you will see that while man likes to insist that woman is fine, delicate, and in need of his care and protection ("Care and protection? Such as the wolf gives the lamb"), he is actually depriving her of all those rights which are "dearer to him than life itself," and over which rivers of blood have been spilled. Then she would look at her questioners with a cold, clear eye and announce flatly that men could not speak for women because they had been educated to believe that women differed materially from themselves, and thus they could not adequately imagine them.

"Moral beings," she explained, "can only judge of others by themselves—the moment they give a different nature to any of their own kind they utterly fail. Let a man once settle the question that woman does not think and feel like himself and he may as well undertake to judge of the amount of intellect and sensation of *any* of the animal creation."

The realization that it was impossible for the men who govern the world to imagine what it felt like to be her came as a thunderbolt: it constituted a second awakening. Before the Seneca Falls convention, she had not truly understood that for men, women were as much another species as blacks were for whites. After the convention— when ridicule and abuse were heaped on the suffragists—she saw not only how deeply the matter went, but that it was of a different nature than she had hitherto suspected. She saw that she was speaking to people who, in the deepest self, did not believe that she was as they were; could not fathom that what was fundamental to their well-being was fundamental to hers. Once she saw this, the perception guided Stanton's thought for the rest of her life, and became the single consideration most responsible for the development in her of intellectual clarity.

Take her famous address to the New York State legislature in 1854, on the eve of the state's constitutional convention. Seneca Falls is well behind her, and she has come to petition, once more, as she has been doing for the past six years and will go on doing for the next fifty, for the redress of woman's grievance under the law.

She reminds the legislators that the majority of American women are native, free-born citizens who hold property, pay taxes, support schools, churches, prisons, the army, the navy, the whole machinery of government, and yet have no voice at all in the shape or course of the life of the nation. In fact, she observes, by the laws of the country women are classed even lower than idiots, lunatics, and negroes: "for the negro can be raised to the dignity of a voter if he possess himself of $250; the lunatic can vote in his moments of sanity; and the idiot too, if he be a male one, and not more than nine tenths a fool."

Speaking to as many elements of legal discrimination as she can—denial of the vote, civil death in marriage, the right to a jury of one's peers, the inequities of widowhood—she lays it all out as though she knows full well that she must work hard to invoke the human empathy that all agree is the proper basis for lawmaking. At last, given everything that she has spoken of, she tells the legislators that it is hardly bearable that they, the suffragists, are forever being asked, in all sobriety, "What exactly is it that you want?"—and cannot help summing up in a passion:

1848

Would to God you could know the burning indignation that fills woman's soul when she thinks of all the beardless boys in your law offices, learning these ideas of one-sided justice—taking their first lessons in contempt for all womankind—being indoctrinated—and to know that these are to be our future presidents, judges, husbands, and fathers . . . In behalf of the women of this state, we ask for all that you have asked for yourselves in the progress of your development since the *Mayflower* cast anchor beside Plymouth rock; and simply on the ground that the rights of every human being are the same and identical.

SUFFRAGE WAS THE UNIVERSITY in which her feeling intelligence was now enrolled, the course of study that encouraged it to deepen and extend itself, the provoking viewpoint that rounded easily on anything in daily life—a book, an encounter, a newspaper story—and quickly brought the waiting rhetoric to a useful boil. From Seneca Falls on—confined to the house as she was, with all those children—hers had become the life of the working radical; plunged into a round of conventions and rallies for which—whether she attended in person or not—she prepared circulars, letters, tracts, articles, speeches written between midnight and dawn; and conducted a correspondence of a strength and volume that could not have been imagined even by her before it became a commonplace.

THIS TRANSFORMATION HAD ACCOMPLISHED ITSELF in her so quickly because one day a few years after the convention Stanton met Susan B. Anthony on a street corner in Seneca Falls. They were introduced casually by mutual friends, and almost immediately there formed between the two women one of the fabled working friendships in

52

American history. Some mysterious chemistry of mind and heart flared instantly between these two, allowing each one, from the very beginning, to speak her every thought in the presence of the other without fear of censure. Also, both saw, and again, very quickly, that each contained within herself the virtues of one half of what was necessary to achieve a sophisticated collaboration: Elizabeth yearned to think and write, Susan to organize and implement. As Stanton put it in her memoirs, she forged the thunderbolts and Anthony fired them.

Of all of the traveling organizers for the movement—and their number multiplied steadily as the years and the decades went by—none compares with Susan Anthony. As Stanton said of her in old age, "There is scarce a town, however small, from New York to San Francisco, that has not heard her ringing voice."

A driven political life—like the life of any professional revolutionary, one that precluded having a home of her own and the emotional nourishment of domestic tranquility—was the one ordained for Susan Anthony. Her family lived in Rochester, where she went often, but she was, in fact, almost always on the road, plunged continually into speaking and organizing tours; especially the latter, for which she had a genius. Anthony could organize anything anywhere anytime. She was famous for being able to arrive in a town in the morning, hire the hall within hours, plaster the place with flyers, and have five hundred people at the meeting in the evening. She organized every national convention for years on end, and could be depended on, not only to solve every problem that arose (from location to speakers to travel arrangements), but also to think of the kinds of details that might preoccupy a director of theatricals. Typical are the instructions contained in a letter she sent to the manager of Washington's Lincoln Hall on January 12, 1875, in preparation for the coming convention:

Do have the hall *floor cleaned* thoroughly—also the *ante rooms*—They were *simply filthy* last year—we had them just after some sort of *tobacco spitting performance*—So please give us every thing clean as silver, and all in real *woman housekeeping* order—& we will not only pay our rent promptly—but say a thousand thanks beside.

Susan Anthony was five years younger than Stanton, a daughter in a large Quaker family, and herself a seasoned worker in reform (mainly temperance and abolition). By 1851 it needed only one or two conversations with Elizabeth Stanton (the chemistry between them was that good) to convert her, utterly and completely and for the rest of her long life, to the urgency of woman suffrage.

In comparison with Stanton, Anthony was complicated: an immensely upright, tightly self-controlled woman embarrassed by any open display of affection or esteem, full of feeling that probably frightened her to death (especially feeling of the senses) and condemned her, on the one hand, to the singleness of life (on which she wrote thoughtfully) but led her, on the other, into the intensely devoted connections she made among three generations of feminists—hundreds of women—for whom she was a beloved figure. She had, it seems, a gift for intimate friendship, and many found it easy to confide in her even though she could not easily do the same. Almost invariably, she was called "Susan" at the start of these friendships, including, of course, the one with Elizabeth Stanton; Anthony, however, called her "Mrs. Stanton" from beginning to end.

But how she prodded Stanton. Year after year after year, Anthony was on her, disapproving of the babies as they came one after another—"For a few moments of pleasure!" she cried in exasperation—but writing endlessly to her, and arriving at her house repeatedly to cajole, "Mrs Stanton, we must have that speech for . . . the teachers

meeting . . . the senate committee . . . this year's convention . . ."
while Stanton laughed good-naturedly, rolled up her sleeves, and sat
down to it, happy to have the excuse of Susan standing over her to
do what in all the world she loved best doing.

Stanton adored testament, and she mastered the art of rhetoric
in order that she might testify with authority. The rich, large-scale
oratory that accompanied every public occasion, solemn or otherwise, was, as Garry Wills observes in *Lincoln at Gettysburg*, "a kind of
performance art with great power over audiences in the middle of
the 19th century . . . an overriding, astonishingly inclusive convention whose moment had arrived in America—where public speakers
hoped to rival Greek drama in creating a people's political identity."
Stanton's articles, addresses, letters, and speeches are an extraordinary
example of how that rhetoric could go to work in an individual with
a talent for it. For instance, this 1854 address of hers to the New
York legislature, of which I have given only a taste, begins,

> The tyrant, Custom, has been summoned before the bar of Common
> Sense. His Majesty no longer awes the multitudes—his scepter is
> broken—his crown is trampled in the dust—the sentence of death is
> pronounced upon him. All nations, ranks and classes have, in turn,
> questioned and repudiated his authority; and now, that the monster is
> chained and caged, timid woman, on tiptoe, comes to look him in the
> face, and to demand of her brave sires and sons, who have struck stout
> blows for liberty, if, in this change of dynasty, she, too, shall find relief.

Then follows a speech that must surely have taken two hours to
deliver (and a number of all-night sessions at the kitchen table to
write). It is hard to know whether Stanton's capaciousness of thought
drove the rhetoric, or the rhetoric stimulated the thought, but her

continually renewed pleasure in laying it all out as fully as possible, in language that makes allusive and anecdotal use, with ease and at length, of history, literature, political and moral philosophy, science and economics, God and the Bible, is unmistakable.

Stanton was not alone among the feminists of her time in thrilling command of oratory—Lucy Stone, Lucretia Mott, the Grimké sisters, and Abby Foster are all known to have stirred the crowd magnificently—but she was one of the best, if not *the* best. For all of these women, oratory was a skill that grew directly out of experience forced on them by their own compelled need to speak—and to be heard. Socrates had said of the art of public speaking, "If you have an innate capacity for rhetoric, you will become a famous rhetorician, provided you also acquire knowledge and practice," adding that if any of the three were missing the project was doomed. Needless to say, none of these women received a course in public speaking at school, nor were they given the opportunity to perform socially. It was only that, driven to champion The Cause—suffrage or temperance or abolition—they soon learned that the gift was theirs; the activist life supplied the remaining two of Socrates' three necessary elements, and they became the astonishing orators they had it in them to become.

The cause, the spirit, the time—and oratory. Living with Stanton, I came to appreciate the fuller meaning of the two- and three-hour speech characteristic of that cause-ridden time. She was, for more than a decade, a speaker on the lyceum circuit, an extraordinary phenomenon in which lecture bureaus booked everything going. This was the American Chautauqua in its prime: a cultural free-for-all unequaled before that time or since. On the circuit, you had hustlers and hypnotists, polemicists and opera singers, medicine men and humorists—as well as every major and minor speaker for abolition, temperance, universal suffrage, and moral transcendentalism, almost every one of whom could deliver a two-hour performance saturated in image and metaphor, reaching back to the classics for the one, and deep into Christianity for the other. Such performances provided excitement and entertainment, major intellectual pleasure, and, often, the only education to be had in rural and small-town America. Imagine hundreds of farmers, housewives, schoolchildren, artisans, shopkeepers, lawyers, and blacksmiths crowding into makeshift meeting halls all over the country; gathered around bandstands, horsecarts, wooden platforms set up out in the open, or under the overhang of a railroad station, or close to a wraparound veranda—all of whom have traveled miles to hear an impassioned exhortation by the speaker on the lyceum circuit on behalf of abolition or Romantic poetry, temperance or Irish home rule, self-reliance or a cure for baldness, women's rights or justice in ancient Athens—and you realize that "silver-tongued oratory" was there to feed hungers of the spirit that went otherwise unrelieved. A short, simple presentation of the matter at hand would never do. Which is why Lincoln's 272-word speech at Gettysburg went magnificently against the grain, and is always seen as an example of greatness making its own terms.

There were many, out on the road, who were simply windbags—what they had to say could easily have been said in half or a quarter of the time they took to say it—delivering rhetoric, indeed, in its most derogatory sense. But for many others, among them Stanton, this habituated practice of immensely long speech-making was intensely fruitful. The practice became Stanton's intellectual home; it not only made her think, it made her educate herself. Each time she wrote a speech, gave a lecture, addressed a convention she saw in her own argument something she hadn't seen before, and some new analogy or simile or metaphor developed that enlarged her understanding and her presentation. There is not a single speech of hers that is a simple repetition of one that came before—with each one the nuance deepens, the insight clarifies, an overlooked example opens a new train of thought, and the air circulating around feeling intelligence is refreshed. She is an artist with a single subject—think Cezanne painting that apple for forty years—continually adding texture, dimension, *essence*, to the body of political thought and feeling that is, ultimately, her masterwork.

Stanton's thoughts, ever concentrated on suffrage, grew steadily more inclusive, leading her not away from devotion to suffrage, but toward the philosophical questions inevitably aroused by revolutionary politics: Why do the injustices matter? What exactly is it that people must fight for? What do these struggles tell us about ourselves? Who *are* we? What do we *need*? How are we meant to be living? In this way, she came—slowly, then quickly—to an eye-opening consideration of something vital affecting the Rights of Man, something that the men who formed the American republic had not taken under consideration but that English radicals of the Enlightenment certainly had: the laws and customs surrounding marriage—and divorce.

Among people like William Godwin, Mary Wollstonecraft, and, later, Robert Owen, the French Revolution had sharpened the conviction that beyond the need for political equality lay an equally great need to create the conditions in which the inner life could flourish. First on the list of their demands was a radical revision of the marriage laws. For these remarkable thinkers, marriage without intimacy—that is, the marriage commonly made without friendship or love out of economic and social considerations—was a prime villain in the matter of stunted or deformed inner lives. They saw that, at best, such arrangements promised neutrality of feeling, and they wrote eloquently to demonstrate that neutrality of feeling is a dangerous illusion: to live without intimacy in the most intimate of circumstances is to sustain permanent damage to the spirit. Forced by law and custom to live in the presence of such an absence, one's inner being closes down—is made cold, defensive, remote—and all too soon one becomes incapable of human empathy: a danger both to oneself and to the world. Godwin and Owen became known as "sexual radicals" as a consequence of writing and speaking endlessly about the death-in-life that is marriage without friendship or love.

Stanton shared the temperament of these radicals and, ultimately, she shared their powerful insight into the crucial desperation of people bound by iron custom (and even-more-iron legality) into a shared circumstance that delivers one over to lifelong spiritual exile. She began by treating marriage mainly as a problem for the political enlightenment of women: "It is in vain to look for the elevation of woman," she said in the 1850s, "so long as she is degraded in marriage . . . [T]he most fatal step a woman can take, the most false of *all earthly relations*, is that under our present legal marriage institution."

Yet she came, over not too many years, to the largest, boldest, most dramatic understanding of any of her contemporaries of what an imprisonment an unhappy marriage is not only for women but for men as well, writing in 1860: "Our marriage is, in many cases, a mere outward tie, impelled by custom, policy, interest, necessity; founded not even in friendship, to say nothing of love . . . Nero was thought the chief of tyrants because he made laws and hung them up so high that his subjects could not read them, and then punished them for every act of disobedience." And she chastised American legislators for making laws that people broke every day through neglect, brutality, and desertion: "To make laws that man cannot and will not obey, serves to bring all law into contempt."

What might help square the law with the reality, she thought, was a marriage contracted for by "equal parties to live an equal life, with equal restraints and privileges on either side." At the end of the decade, in 1869, she was confirmed in this thought by none other than John Stuart Mill; she observed with pleasure that one third of the newly published *Subjection of Women* "is devoted to the marriage relation, and Mr. Mill clearly shows that on a complete reconstruction of this institution on the *basis of equality* depends the regeneration of the race."

But even this—equality in the marriage laws—she came to think inadequate. In October of 1874, with the entire country continuing to be mesmerized by the unfolding scandal of the adulterous affair between Henry Beecher and Elizabeth Tilton—tabloids being grabbed every day out of newsboys' hands by low- and high-minded alike— Stanton warned:

> To compel unhappy husbands and wives, by law and public sentiment, to live together, and to teach them that it is their religious duty to accept their conditions, whatever they are, produces, ever and anon, just such social earthquakes as the one through which we are now passing. If all our homes were unroofed, many a husband might be painted in darker colors than Theodore Tilton, and many a wife weaker than his, and many a man more perplexed and miserable than "the Great Preacher." Hence we have, all alike, a deeper interest in this "scandal" than the guilt or innocence of the actors.

Stanton thought hard about the effect of an unhappy marriage on the human spirit because her own marriage, while not unhappy, was not happy. Henry Stanton had, after all, turned out not a soulmate. He did not forbid her her life (no mean thing for a man of his time), but divisions of thought and feeling between them grew with every passing year. In this couple those divisions took the form of political disagreement. Before the war, Henry supported political antislavery while Elizabeth was a passionate Garrisonian; after the war he supported the Republican stand on Reconstruction, while she mounted a raging campaign against the antifeminist Fourteenth and Fifteenth Amendments. He could not bear the heat of her radicalism, she could not bear the lukewarmth of his expediency. In a sense the connection between them remained amiable—Elizabeth once wrote that she and Henry continued to laugh together and to enjoy reading the morning paper together throughout their shared life—but I think it safe to say that fifteen years into the forty they more or less spent together the marriage no longer engaged her. As Emerson wrote in 1840, the very year the Stantons were married, "*Do you love me?* means at last *Do you see the same truth I see?* If you do, we are happy together; but when presently one of us passes into the perception of a new truth, we are divorced and the force of all nature cannot hold us to each other." In September of 1869, in a surprising letter to fellow feminist Isabella Hooker, Stanton laid out the case more clearly:

Like you I hate to leave a quiet pleasant home, it is a great trial to me to leave my quiet retreat, children and husband. As to the latter, I fear from our conversation you may imagine my domestic relations not altogether happy. I have no doubt they are far more so than 99/100 of married people ... Mr. Stanton is a highly cultivated liberal man; hence we are one in our literary tastes. He is a very cheerful, sunny, genial man, hence we can laugh together. His health is perfect, hence we can walk and eat together. He loves music, so do I, he loves oratory so do I, he is interested in all political questions so am I. But our theology [ideology] is as wide apart as the north and south pole so we never talk on all those points where we both feel most. My views trouble him. I accept his philosophically, knowing that certain organizations [psychological constitutions] and educations must produce certain results. If he could do the same we should be nearer and dearer I have no doubt.

That was as far as she could go. After this she writes, "But it is as bad to read long letters as to write them—this from a woman who routinely wrote letters as long as articles!—so I will not tax your brain with those things we shall talk over many times this side of the Jordan." One doubts that they ever did.

So here they were, Elizabeth and Henry, two of the most decent, freethinking, privileged people in America, with each one extending the other a remarkable amount of personal freedom—yet happiness eluded them. Marriage left each of them drifting about inside an isolation of the spirit that, in time, grew oppressive (and indeed, as the years went on, they came to live more and more apart). Out of this emptiness in her own life, Stanton's thinking took an empathetic leap, allowed her to imagine fully a life trapped inside a *really* soul-deadening marriage. Better, far better, she realized, to be alone, than to face daily the intolerable loneliness that one experienced in the presence of the absence. The laws regarding marriage *and* divorce had to be altered.

It grew and grew in her that she must speak out for divorce. But every time she opened her mouth on the subject, everyone around her demurred, "No, no, the time is not right. It will harm the woman's movement." She balked at being told the time was not right. If one sees that a thing is true, she thought, the time is *always* right to express it. How can speaking the truth harm the movement, ever?

Yet she let it go, speaking out only here and there—the first time in an article in the feminist newspaper the *Lily*, in April 1850, where she concentrated safely enough on the temperance argument— namely that divorce be granted a woman on the basis of having a drunkard for a husband. She not only thought drunkenness a ground for divorce, she said; she thought a law should be passed forbidding drunkards to marry.

In the summer of 1853 she again felt impelled to speak. In correspondence with Lucy Stone, she said that she wanted to place divorce on the agenda of the upcoming woman's rights convention in Cleveland, but Stone wrote to dissuade her, saying,

> I do not think, let Truth come from what source it may, that any one has a right to *keep* it. But I do think, that a premature announcement of it, is possible. As Jesus said, "I have many things to tell you, but *hitherto*, ye were not able to bear it" . . . I think that we agree, in all, except it be the *time* to strike. I shall be glad to get your thoughts for there is not another woman in our ranks who thinks or who dares speak what she thinks on this topic, so far as I know.

It is unlikely that they actually did agree on the subject. Most reformers thought that drunkenness should be allowable as a reason for divorce, along with impotence or adultery (the only other causes that stood up in court), but only Stanton carried the question of divorce to the deeper level of spiritual misalliance.

The Tenth National Woman's Rights Convention was held at the Cooper Institute (now Cooper Union) in New York City on May 10 and 11, 1860. A thousand people attended. Martha Wright was the presiding officer, Susan B. Anthony reported on the year's work,

Wendell Phillips delivered an impressive argument for woman suffrage, and Elizabeth Stanton repeated the address she had delivered
to the New York legislature in March of that year.

Only two days before, on May 8, Stanton had addressed the
American Anti-Slavery Society from the same stage (the Cooper Institute did an extraordinary amount of business in those years with
radical and reformist conventions). Invited, for the first time, by Garrison, to address the society, she was aware of the delicacy of the
situation—the audience filled with friends and associates whom she
did not wish to alienate—yet, like every radical ever born, she could
not speak but to grind her own axe. She reminded the society of its
own motto—"The world is my country and all mankind my coun-
trymen"—and told of how these sentiments had affected her
thought and development as a feminist: "I shall never forget our
champions in [London in 1840]: how noble Phillips did speak, and
how still more nobly Garrison would not speak because woman was
there denied her rights." The anti-slavery movement, she said, had
been an education of the first order. It had taught her to take the
long view—"In spite of noble words, deeds of thirty years of
protest, prayers and preaching, slavery still lives"—but the important
thing about these long, hard years of political work was that "in the
discussion of this question, how many of us have worked out our
salvation: what mountains of superstition have been rolled off the
human soul!" Then she cleverly led the speech to the place where she
could say, "Eloquently and earnestly as noble men have denounced
slavery on this platform . . . a privileged class can never conceive the
feelings of those who are born to contempt, to inferiority, to degradation. Herein is woman more fully identified with the slave than
man can possibly be, for she can take the subjective view"; and con-

cluded that the slave who is a woman combines in her person "the highest degree of degradation known to organized human life."

What a thorn in her side this organization, and these men, had been for twenty years now. The self-assurance with which they determined the agenda of reform. The dominating character of their views. The subtle discounting of the woman's movement. All the while complaining that the movement was so disappointing—its lack of boldness, organization, progress. Above all: boldness.

Now, on the second day of the Tenth Woman's Rights Convention, she carried out her intention—announced in private to her colleagues, and much protested by them—to speak about marriage and divorce. She began by presenting a number of resolutions, arguing first and foremost that an "ill-assorted" marriage is a calamity, not a crime; that any covenant between human beings that failed to produce or promote human happiness not only had no force or authority, but a positive duty to abolish itself; that it was an insult and a mockery to claim physical impotence a sufficient cause for divorce while no amount of mental, moral, or spiritual anguish is considered sufficient; that daily observation and experience show how incompetent people are at choosing partners in business, teachers for their children, ministers of their religion, and administrators of their laws, so why not admit that the same incompetence often applies in choosing a husband or a wife; and, finally, that a child born of "unhappy and unhallowed connections" is destined to develop the kind of depraved nature that ensures the human race will continue to weaken itself to the point of bringing on its own ruin—"a just penalty of long-violated law."

Stanton then delivered a speech in which she acknowledged that it was, indeed, the inequities in marriage between women and men that had first drawn her attention: "[After all], a man can marry and not change his life one iota . . . but in marriage, woman gives up all." And should the husband turn out badly, "today so noble, so generous, [but] in a few short years transformed into a cowardly, mean tyrant, or a foul-mouthed, bloated drunkard," then what? (Ironically, within twenty years the English novelist George Gissing would, in novel after novel, be describing marriage in exactly the same terms, except for Gissing the woman is always the villain. "Who could have imagined," his collective protagonist is forever reflecting, "that within five years the lovely, adoring girl he had married with such high hopes would emerge as this ignorant, nagging slattern who made of his days and nights an unending hell, and to whom he was shackled for life"?)

When Stanton had done speaking, the whole convention fell into tumult and argument. Antoinette Blackwell, the great feminist preacher, in a lengthy statement, opposed divorce categorically, claiming that marriage "must be, from the nature of things, as permanent as the life of the parties" and that "all divorce is naturally and morally impossible," although she agreed with Stanton that the laws as they now stood made the subjection of women integral to the enterprise of marriage. Ernestine Rose replied tartly that Blackwell had delivered a long lecture about what "ought to be" but that, the world being what it is, divorce should be made readily available to mitigate what now *is*. Wendell Phillips objected to the whole discussion, claiming it had no place in a women's rights meeting, where talk should be limited to "the laws that rest unequally upon women, not those that rest equally upon men and women." William Lloyd Garrison demurred, in measured tones, that marriage, he believed, was "at least incidental to the main question of equal rights of woman." Antoinette Blackwell then took the floor one last time to make clear that the question of marriage "*must* come upon this platform" because it bears unequally upon women—but not divorce. After this, Susan Anthony, in total agreement with Stanton but ever the political organizer struggling to avoid conflict within the ranks, then smoothly wrapped things up, saying only that she sincerely hoped Wendell Phillips hadn't meant it when he'd said he thought these resolutions should be stricken from the record of this convention. Obviously, a rock had been overturned from beneath which crawled the worm of a very live, very anxiety-provoking issue.

Every one of the nineteenth-century women's rights conventions, both national and state, was attended by the press and almost always thoroughly reported on, with the text of the proceedings appearing in part or in whole in the newspapers. Stanton's resolutions on divorce at this one sent the New York press into a tailspin. The *Evening Post* warned that people would be disgusted with equating marriage with a business contract. (A hundred years later, in 1969, when Alix Kates Shulman voiced exasperation about domestic inequity in the essay "A Marriage Agreement," the same objection was raised!) The *Tribune* called these ideas "simply shocking" and marveled "that a modest woman should say" what Stanton had said. The *Herald* found it "difficult to believe that the speakers were females" and accused them of preaching revolt. The *New York Observer* announced that no true woman could listen to what had been said without turning scarlet, yet words that "would turn the world into one vast brothel" had been read "unblushingly by a person in woman's attire, named in the programme as Mrs. Elizabeth Cady Stanton."

Once again, Stanton—always amazed when her pronouncements were received as anything less than the simplest and most obvious of truths—felt stung by the rebuking response, not only in the

press but at the convention itself, and among conservative feminists
at large. When Caroline Dall wrote haughtily in Garrison's newspaper, *The Liberator*, that "the women of Boston regard a present consideration of the subject of Marriage and Divorce as premature and
unwise," Stanton shot back,

> If to anyone is given a clear perception of an egregious wrong . . . *now*
> is always the time to cry aloud and spare not. Perhaps the American na-
> tion thought the "Printer's Boy" [Garrison] "premature and unwise"
> when, thirty years ago, he proclaimed the doctrine of "immediate and
> unconditional emancipation," for even the friends of the slave who
> gathered round him stood appalled at the boldness and rashness of his
> declaration.

But it was Wendell Phillips's reprimand that hurt the most. Stanton wrote angrily to Susan B., "With all his excellence and nobility
Wendell Phillips is a man. His words, tone, and manner came down
on me like a clap of thunder. We are right, however. My reason, my
experience, my soul proclaims it." And to Martha Wright she wrote
defensively, "Those sad-faced women who struggled up to press my
hand, who were speechless with emotion, know better than the greatest of our masculine speakers and editors who has struck the blow
for them in the right place. I shall trust my instinct and my reason
until some masculine logic meets mine better than it has yet done
on the point at issue."

For all her dismay, the brouhaha exhilarated Stanton—"Fear not
that I shall falter," she ends a letter to Susan B. "I shall not grow conservative with age. I feel a growing indifference to the praise and
blame of my race"—and the passion over divorce did not abate. It

was, for her, a matter of inspired urgency, one that allowed her to feel, acutely and repeatedly, the pathos of the human condition.

In November of 1869 a man named Daniel McFarland shot a journalist named Albert Richardson in the offices of the New York *Tribune*. Abby McFarland had left her abusive husband in New York, divorced him secretly in Indiana, and was planning to marry Richardson. Now, as Richardson lay dying at home, he and Abby were married, and a tremendous outcry of "Sacrilege!" was heard throughout the country. McFarland, indicted for murder, was acquitted of his crime on the grounds of insanity—and then given custody of the children!

At a mass meeting of women in New York—the hall was packed—Stanton spoke out on McFarland's acquittal. The absorbed interest of the country in the trial, she said, proved that the question of marriage and divorce was a momentous one, involving the whole of our social, religious, and political life. As for herself, she thought that divorce "at the will of the parties is not only right, but that it is a sin against nature, the family, the State, for a man or a woman to live together in the marriage relation in continual antagonism, indifference, disgust. A physical union should be the outgrowth of a spiritual and intellectual sympathy; and anything short of this is lust and not love."

Not only did *she* think this, she went on heatedly, but so did Jeremy Bentham: "A condition requiring a continuance of marriage notwithstanding a change in the feelings of the parties is absurd, shocking, and contrary to humanity"; Charlotte Bronte: "When a wife's nature loathes that of the man she is wedded to, marriage must be slavery; against slavery all right thinkers revolt . . . for freedom is indispensable"; John Stuart Mill: "The subject of marriage is usually discussed as if the interests of children were everything, those of grown persons nothing"; and Charles Dickens: "I read [regularly] in the papers . . . how the impossibility of ever getting unchained from one another at any price on any terms brings blood upon the land."

It would have been better, Stanton added, if Abby McFarland had openly demanded a divorce and obtained it in the State of New York—that would be *her* idea of true reform, "not to coquette with unjust law, thrust it to one side, or try to get beyond its reach, but to fight it where it is, and fight it to the death"—and concluded by urging "the women of this state to rise in mass and say they will no longer tolerate statutes" that hold unhappy women and men indissolubly bound to one another.

She had opinions on everything, and the newspapers of her day (both mainstream and radical), along with letters, journals, and diary entries, allowed her to air them nonstop. Reading through Stanton's many short newspaper pieces we catch a glimpse of the kind of indiscriminate liveliness that so often lies behind the focused passions of a personality as strong as hers.

She always felt that waging revolution without living fully while one was at it was worse than useless. In this, she strongly resembles Fanny Wright, Mary Wollstonecraft, Rosa Luxemburg, Emma Goldman, and Margaret Sanger, all of whom led bold, independent-minded, sexually adventurous lives throughout their politically active years. Stanton's life, however, was intensely domesticated, and while she was sexually vigorous she was also an upper-class American innocent: not for nothing the grandmotherly image acquired in early middle age. For her, living fully meant responding to the stream of daily event. Nothing was too insignificant to gain or hold her attention—which, inevitably, combined the domestic with the political with the social with the anecdotal (here, Anthony, who wished her to concentrate on speech-making, could not make a dent). She loved nothing better than letting it all tumble together. "Dear Liz," she writes in 1851 to her great intimate, Gerrit Smith's daughter, Libby Miller,

> Have you any flower seeds for a body, especially mignonette? . . . How do you manage mumps, whooping cough? The spirits seem to be making some new manifestations! [She is referring to the séance "rappings" then popular among their friends.] I am convinced that it is all humbug. How strange, is it not, that these very minds which reject Christ and his miracles and all the mysteries of the Bible, because these things are opposed to reason and the truth as we see it in other revelations of God's laws, should be deluded by this miserable piece of chicanery! There's nothing more wonderful about it than the performance of a necromancer. Have sent my letter to Salem [a long recommendation for amending the Ohio state constitution in favor of women's rights].

For many years, all she had had by way of keeping her mind alive was intelligent application to the homely problems of family life. In her memoir she tells us that four days after the birth of her first child it was discovered that he had a bent collarbone. The doctors devised a bandage around the wrist to apply pressure to the shoulder. The baby's hand turned blue. Stanton applied herself to the problem and devised another sort of bandage—one that went over the shoulders like a set of suspenders, crossing them both in front and in back— and at the end of ten days the bone had righted itself. The doctors smiled at each other and one of them said, "Well, after all, a mother's instinct is better than a man's reason." She replied, "Thank you, gentlemen, there was no instinct about it. I did some hard thinking before I saw how I could get a pressure on the shoulder without impeding the circulation, as you did." Of this episode, she writes: "I learned a lesson in self-reliance. I trusted neither men nor books absolutely after this . . . but continued to use my 'mother's instinct' if 'reason' is too dignified a term to apply to woman's thoughts." Against all the prevailing wisdom, Stanton became a devotee of loose clothing and wide-open windows at night.

Indeed, one of her passions was reform in women's dress (enveloped as women were, from the cradle to the grave, in masses of floor-length material) and in women's hair styles (always a heavy accumulation on top of one's head). In 1852, having cut off her own long hair, in a piece in the *Lily* called "James, the Barber" she urges the same on her readers:

> He has just had a room neatly fitted up for ladies—where he will cut off the hair and shampoo the head for the small sum of one shilling [a coin worth twelve and a half cents]. It would delight all physiologists and lovers of comfort, to see the heaps of beautiful curls and rich braids that have fallen beneath James's magic touch, from the over heated aching heads of about one dozen of our fair ones. If all the women could know the luxury of short hair, there would soon be a general leave taking of hair-pins, combs, braids and knots.

More despairing by far was the question of skirts that swept the dust. In 1851, the editor of the Seneca County *Courier* wrote critically of women's dress. Amelia Bloomer, a resident of Seneca Falls, replied challengingly, in the *Lily*, that women might take to wearing trousers, and the editor then dared her to practice what she preached. Bloomer did just that, creating the Bloomer costume (a skirt halfway down the leg worn over harem pants); whereupon, Stanton wrote a piece in the *Lily* in which she invoked a character she called Sobriny Jane:

Some time ago, dear reader, I told you about my cousin Sobriny Jane . . . I had always thought that Sobriny was sensitive to public sentiment; too much so, ever to strike out for herself a new path, unaided and alone. But of late the very spirit of [the moment] seems to have inspired her anew. During the short cold days of December . . . she assembled together her whole inheritance of petticoats, and, by a skillful surgical operation, separated those parts which were forever groveling in the dust, from those nearest the heart. She then slipped her neatly turned foot and ankle into a masculine boot, leaped into a pair of Turkish trowsers, and walked forth a mile and a half, through sleet and snow . . . Sobriny prophecies that henceforth the votaries of Fashion shall worship at a Turkish shrine; for the French having proved themselves incapable of forming a model Republic, are of necessity unfit to invent costumes worthy of imitation [by] daughters of the Pilgrim Fathers . . .

Three years later, however, after many of the feminists had tried wearing the Bloomer costume and been hooted at in the street, in the middle of that year's women's rights convention in Washington, Susan B. received a letter from Lucy Stone saying that Stone dreaded going into another meeting wearing the Bloomer costume. As Anthony sat writing in reply, Stanton seized the letter and added a passage of her own: "Lucy, I have but a moment to say, for your own sake, lay aside the shorts. I know what you suffer among fashionable people. Not for the sake of the cause, nor for any sake but your own, take it off. We put the dress on for greater freedom, but what is physical freedom compared with mental bondage? By all means have the new dress made long." (Thirty years after that, when Stanton and Stone were sworn enemies, Stanton was sent an article that had appeared in Lucy Stone's *Woman's Journal*, written by a woman who'd been young at the Seneca Falls convention. The article remembered Stanton in those years as "stout, short, with her merry eye and expression of great good humor" but as one who made the writer think that no scarecrow had ever been "better calculated to scare all the birds, beasts and human beings than was Mrs. Stanton in the Bloomer dress.")

Another of her passions was the slavery of housekeeping. She knew how many women had no gift for it at all, and that their lives were a misery of daily domestic chaos. Everything about the situation—including the bad housekeepers themselves—exasperated her. On this issue, she tartly instructed the readers of the *Lily* to "have one place for everything, and train your household to put things in their proper places. Then husband, children and servants can all wait on themselves."

Meanwhile, her own house was a hotel. Almost everyone—in abolition or women's rights—who ever came through Seneca Falls slept at the Stantons'. One can't help wondering: What on earth. With all those children. But Susan B. hastens (in Stanton's obituary, no less) to *assure* us that she was an excellent housekeeper.

She had opinions—and she had mortifications.

In 1856 her pregnancies still amused her. Half a year after the birth of her sixth child, in response to a frantic plea of Anthony's— where are you? why don't you answer my letters? I need you to write a speech—she replies cheerfully,

Your servant is not dead but liveth . . . day in and day out, watching, bathing, dressing, nursing and promenading the precious contents of a little crib in the corner of my room . . . Is your speech to be exclusively on the point of educating the sexes together, or as to the best manner of educating women? Have you Horace Mann on that point? Come

here and I will do what I can to help you with your address, if you will
hold the baby and make the puddings . . .

Two years later she had lost her sense of humor.

In 1858, in the middle of her last and most difficult pregnancy
(she was now forty-three years old), she had become the first woman
to be invited to lecture in Boston's prestigious Fraternity Lecture
Course—and at that, in a season that included Emerson and the
great theologian Theodore Parker. At the very last minute she can-
celled, giving the theft of a trunk as her lame excuse. Every feminist,
including Susan B., was deeply irritated. To her cousin, Libby, she
wrote the truth:

> Why did I not fulfill my engagement in Boston? In all other pregnan-
> cies, the fifth month usually finds me in excellent health but this one
> differed from all its antecedents. I grew worse instead of better—sick,
> nervous, timid, and so short-breathed that it was impossible for me to
> read one page aloud . . . I selected the trunk episode as an excuse. I
> could not give the other to strangers . . . as the maternal difficulty has
> always been one of the arguments against women entering public life.
> I did not like the idea that I, who had a hundred times declared that
> difficulty to be absurd, should illustrate in my own person the contrary
> thesis. It was all too humiliating to be disclosed . . . I hope I shall never
> meet on earth Mr. Slack [secretary of the Lecture Course]; in heaven
> he could appreciate the nicety of the case.

That same year, exhausted and in a rare bitter moment, she
writes to Anthony: "When I pass the gate of the celestials and good
Peter asks me where I wish to sit, I will say, 'Anywhere so that I am
neither a negro nor a woman.'"

An absence of political empathy between the feminists and those they wanted to consider their comrades ate into her spirit, and made flare her considerable capacity for reckless anger. In such a mood, she defends an account of domestic tyranny called *Ruth Hall: A Domestic Tale of the Present Time* against a negative review in the *Anti-Slavery Standard* in 1855:

> We were sorry to see so severe a review in an anti slavery paper. It was unworthy a place there, in columns that profess so much sympathy for humanity. The heart, if you have one, does sometimes hold the head in abeyance. Read *Ruth Hall* as you would read the life of a Frederick Douglass, as you would listen to the poor slaves in our anti-slavery meetings. The story of cruel wrongs, suffered for weary days and years, finds sympathy in every breast. What is grammar, or rhetoric, rules of speech or modes of thought, when a human soul pours forth his tale of woe to his fellow man! . . . The next mulatto slave that comes North, and gets upon a platform, to tell of the cruelty and injustice of his father and brethren, hiss him down—read him the laws on "filial reverence," tell him his speech has no literary merit, "that he had better turn his attention to something else than oratory."

The men who were the self-declared friends of women's rights gave her grief everlasting. Some, of course, were brilliantly loyal throughout their lives, but for many others, interest and support sprang up early while disappointment and disaffection seemed to set in just as early. Each one thought that the woman's movement should make *his* idea of timely progress, and when it failed to do so, became disenchanted.

Typical of those who applauded the suffragists early but who also lost heart early was Thomas Wentworth Higginson (abolition-

ist, literary man, Civil War hero), who had, in 1850, said euphori-
cally, "Now the logic is all with the women," but ten years later was
writing to Stanton,

> I had always taken the ground that the acquiescence of the vast ma-
> jority of women was like that of slaves, but observation has taught me
> that no such phenomenon is to be found among slaves. The ac-
> quiescence of women—for it is not an unwilling, coerced, dogged
> submission—is an argument hard to answer *for a man*. Certainly men
> can never secure women's rights vicariously for them. Hence a sort of
> chill of discouragement.

A few years later Wendell Phillips was making the same point:
"The singularity of this cause," he said, "is that it has to be argued
against the wishes and purposes of its victims."

Even more painfully, as early as December of 1855, Gerrit
Smith had written an open letter to Stanton (in Frederick Douglass's
North Star), in which he explained that he no longer had faith in the
woman's movement that he had once held in high regard—this is just
seven years after Seneca Falls!—because he simply did not see
enough progress: "The mass of women . . . are content in their help-
lessness and poverty and destitution of rights," he writes, and the
leaders are content to wear "a dress which imprisons and cripples
them . . . that both marks and makes their impotence." If women
would simply refuse to wear what they are told to wear, men would
begin to take them seriously as equals.

Stanton, pregnant at the time of Smith's letter, wrote to Martha
Wright that she wanted to consult with her before sending her reply.
"As I am rather larger than you," Stanton added, "suppose you come
to me instead of my going to you. Come over in the first train some

morning this week and we will criticize together. Two heads are better than one, especially when one head is full of baby clothes & labor
pains. I have a month grace still, yours in haste." And in this state she
wrote a ten-page reply to Smith, assuring him that "the mass of
women are developed at least to the point of discontent and *that*, in
the dawn of this nation, was considered a most dangerous point in
the British Parliament, and is now deemed equally so on a southern
plantation." However, she reminds him, "public sentiment and the religion of our day teach us that silence is most becoming in a woman,"
and this is a tremendous force, long internalized, that makes it more
difficult than he can ever truly grasp for women to speak out, loudly
and clearly, as quickly as he, and she, would wish them to. On the
matter of dress, she points out that once men dressed like women,
and the skirt hadn't made a damned bit of difference—"Was the old
Roman in his toga less of a man than he is now in swallow-tail and
tights? Did the flowing robes of Christ himself render his life less
grand and beautiful?"—and she argues that women must *first* stand
on "an even pedestal with man" and *then* "shall our efforts at minor
reforms be crowned with complete success."

History, of course, has debated this equation many times. Smith
says, You won't be free until you stop wearing long skirts and mile-
wide crinolines. Stanton replies, We can't stop wearing them until we
are free. The real stumbling block, though, is that either way nothing
can be achieved until a critical mass is reached, and in 1855 that was
nowhere near in sight. At the end of her letter, Stanton urged Smith
to renewed faith, assuring him that "when the mass of women see
that there is some hope of becoming voters and law-makers, they
will take to their rights as naturally as the Negro to his heels when he
is sure of success."

But it all stuck in her craw—how shallow was their understand-

ing, how weak their allegiance—so that when it came to facing down
these men at the end of the Civil War, as they made unequivocally
clear that they would concentrate on gaining suffrage for black men
only, there was, quite simply, nothing for her to think about.

In May of 1863, in New York City, in the middle of the war,
Stanton and Anthony helped found the Women's Loyal National
League, which, at a series of meetings, kept hammering away at the
need for the nation to address women's disenfranchisement as well as
the negro's once the shooting stopped. But when the shooting did
stop, although there were men and women in the abolitionist movement who *were* torn apart by the guilty conviction that now they
should throw their weight behind universal suffrage, political expedience told them that suffrage for women would never carry the day,
and persuaded them to abandon the struggle altogether.

During the summer and fall of 1865, while the question of
suffrage—for whom? and under what conditions?—is occupying the
entire country, Stanton throws down the gauntlet in article after
article:

> The question for today is not how or where to limit the right of suf-
> frage, but where did the privileged few get their power to deprive the
> masses of their inalienable right to life, liberty, and the pursuit of hap-
> piness? . . . The cool impudence of these pirates in civil rights, who
> look in the faces of disenfranchised citizens and talk of the dangers of
> extending the privileges they claim for themselves, is only equaled by
> the boldness of their reasoning . . .
>
> No country ever has had or ever will have peace until every citizen
> has a voice in the government. Now let us try universal suffrage. We
> cannot tell its dangers or delights until we make the experiment. At all
> events, let us leave behind the dead skin of class legislation . . .

The struggle of the last thirty years has not been merely on the black man as such, but on the broader ground of his humanity. Our Fathers, at the end of the first revolution, in their desire for a speedy readjustment of all their difficulties, and in order to present to Great Britain, their common enemy, an united front, accepted the compromise urged on them by South Carolina, and a century of wrong, ending in another revolution [the Civil War is always called a revolution], has been the result of their action . . . This is our opportunity to retrieve the errors of the past and mould anew the elements of Democracy.

In January of 1866, when she still had reason to hope that the abolitionists were with her, she wrote to Gerrit Smith to beg him to oppose a resolution that had been introduced in Congress, one that proposed congressional representation based on the number of male citizens over the age of twenty-one in a given district, reminding him that "as our Constitution now exists there is nothing to prevent women or negroes from holding the ballot, but if that word 'male' be inserted as now proposed, it will take us a century at least to get it out again." Smith did not reply.

Every abolitionist she had ever worked with was outraged at her position, including feminists like Lucy Stone, who broke irrevocably with Stanton over the point. One and all implored her to understand that the turn of women would come, but right now it was "the negro's hour." To no avail. The woman who had only the year before written to Wendell Phillips, "When we forsake principle for expediency all is doubt & bewilderment" was not about to back down now—not for anyone.

It is here, at this exact moment in history, that the meaning of radical feminism in America is established; here, in fact, that it consolidates, separates itself from the liberal feminism that, in the face of legitimate conflict, attenuates its analysis and draws back from going an uncompromising limit that threatens to set us all on a road of no return. Throw down *this* gauntlet, it is felt by the liberal, and the world as we know it goes under or changes beyond recognition: either way, a fearful prospect. *Refuse* to throw down this gauntlet, says the radical feminist, and not only is the true nature of women's rights obscured, but also all hope of success is painfully compromised (in the end, of course, the radical prevails only by inching the liberal forward—a generation later).

At that terrible moment of social triage in 1867, "either everyone walks through the door or no one walks through the door" was a position deplored by almost everyone Stanton knew: a moment of heartbreaking impasse for all concerned. Those who had worked their guts out for abolition, over thirty years and more, never dreaming that they would see slavery come to an end in their lifetime, now found it impossible to swallow hard and say (as she said, and kept on saying), "Votes for all or votes for none." Elizabeth Stanton understood the anxieties of her moment all too well, but she herself was now in the grip of a need that superseded all others.

In a remarkable passage in *Democracy in America*, Alexis de Tocqueville observes that for the past four centuries equality rather than freedom is what men and women the world over have been driving toward. What people "love with an eternal love," he insists, is equality. He makes the distinction between equality and freedom by observing that the hunger for freedom is an impulse and an effort that flares up and dies down—if unsuccessful, resignation sets in—but to live without equality, once one is *conscious* that one is living without it, is a condition to which none can resign themselves; and very often a people demonstrates that it would rather "perish than to lose it." Whether de Tocqueville's distinction is legitimate—for many freedom and equality are an equivalent—it is certainly true that at the end of the Civil War, Elizabeth Stanton found herself gazing with unsentimental eyes and a newly hardened heart at the disintegrating hope of universal suffrage—her sine qua non of equality—and now, in 1867, she very nearly was ready to see civilization as she knew it go under, rather than continue living without it.

To take a look at the valiant efforts made by some on behalf of the larger ideal is to have instantly revealed the impassioned confusion that, throughout the 1860s, kept many good people ricocheting off the wall of universal suffrage onto that of manhood suffrage, and back again:

At the Eleventh Women's Rights Convention in New York in May of 1866 (with Stanton presiding) a group of sufficiently like-minded abolitionists and suffragists agreed that the women's rights convention, as such, would dissolve into a newly created organization to be called the American Equal Rights Association, now formed for the specific purpose of trying to see whether they *could* work together for universal suffrage. At the association's opening meeting, the New Hampshire abolitionist Stephen Foster spoke for many when he said emotionally,

> The question for every man and woman, now, is the rights of all men and women . . . I could not ask woman to go up and down the length and breadth of the land demanding the political recognition of any class of disenfranchised citizens, while her own rights are ignored . . . I have demanded the freedom of the slave the last thirty years because he was a human being, and I now demand suffrage for the negro because he is a human being, and for the same reason I demand the ballot for woman. Therefore, our demand for this hour is equal suffrage to all

disfranchised classes, for the one and the same reason—they are all human beings.

One year later, however, at the association's first anniversary meeting, the previously unacknowledged divisions within even *this* association surfaced in full strength. Right off, George Downing wants to know "whether he had rightly understood that Mrs. Stanton and Mrs. Mott were opposed to the enfranchisement of the colored man, unless the ballot should also be accorded to woman at the same time." Stanton tells him, Yes, he has understood rightly. Stephen Foster now seems to reverse himself, saying he feels "bound to confer it [suffrage] on any citizen deprived of it irrespective of its being granted or denied to others." Abby Kelley Foster agrees. If the negro and the woman were in the same civil, social, and political status today she would support universal suffrage but as they are not . . . The Reverend Samuel May demurs that he himself is "of the opinion that by asking for the rights of all, we should be much more likely to obtain the rights of the colored man, than by making that a special question." George Downing demands that the group be resolved that it "favors the enfranchisement of the colored man."

Elizabeth Stanton repeats that she demands the ballot for all.

Then she gets on her elitist high horse, and says that "if we are to have further class legislation then let it be on the basis of education . . . Only educated men should be allowed to vote . . . Why ask educated women, who love their country, who desire to mould its institutions on the highest idea of justice and equality, who feel that their enfranchisement is of vital importance to this end, why ask them to stand aside while two million ignorant men are ushered into the halls of legislation?"

Abby Foster cries out, "Shame! Shame! Shame!"

The black abolitionist Charles Lennox Remond now repudiates expediency, announcing, "All I ask for myself I claim for my wife and sister. Let our action be based upon the rock of everlasting principle." After all this—and more—Susan Anthony reads out two telegrams from Lucy Stone and Sam Wood (a Kansas senator), on the road together, campaigning for a pair of separate amendments for black suffrage and woman suffrage that are up for ratification in Kansas. At this moment they think victory within their reach. Stone's telegram reads: "Impartial Suffrage, *without regard to color or sex*, will succeed by overwhelming majorities. Kansas rules the world!" Sam Wood's: "With the help of God and Lucy Stone, we shall carry Kansas! The world moves." But they didn't—and it didn't. Campaigning abolitionists ditched the feminist amendment to assure suffrage for black men. In the end, both were defeated, exactly as Stanton had predicted that, if pitted against one another, they would be.

By October of that year (1867), Stanton and Anthony were themselves campaigning in Kansas ("enduring terrible roads, inedible food, and bedbugs") where, to their mutual horror, they witnessed the American political circus at its uninhibited worst—a ruthless trading of votes for one amendment or the other going on everywhere—and saw as well how ignorant most women were about what was at stake: ignorant and narrow in a way that seemed to far exceed the narrowness of their men.

It was then—running out of every kind of resource—that, in anger, exhaustion, and an acute sense of abolitionist betrayal, they decided to accept the support and patronage of George Francis Train, a rich, racist maverick from Boston whose odd assortment of causes included the eight-hour day for labor, Irish home rule, inflationary currency—and woman suffrage. Train's style was disruptive and flamboyant, his speech brilliant and more than slightly mad, and he was roundly loathed by abolitionists one and all.

George Train supported a three-month speaking tour for Stanton and Anthony from Kansas to New York, at the end of which the American Equal Rights Association had estranged itself from them, and Lucy Stone—along with many other appalled feminists—was made into an implacable, lifelong enemy. Ten years earlier, when Stone, for whom abolition was a religious crusade, was already becoming apprehensive about Stanton's willingness to place women's rights at the absolute center of the movement's concerns, she had written to Susan B.,

> Mrs. Stanton, God bless her! She is partly right, and partly wrong— the *resentment* at the injustice, and meanness, is all right, but the serving the *highest right, for the sake of the right, whatever* may come to us, is still our duty, and the surest way, by its example of nobility, to teach men that we are fully worthy to be copartners with them in everything. The cause of Kansas [ever the important border state], and of the country are still *our cause,* even though we *are* disenfranchised . . . So, it is for *our interest,* to aid in securing justice for Kansas.

Now, sure enough, just as Stone had all along feared, Stanton and Anthony had done the unforgivable. When, subsequently, the National Woman Suffrage Association was formed (with Stanton as president), Stone would take many of their formerly united colleagues with her into the rival American Woman Suffrage Association. To the detriment of women's rights, the two organizations would work independent of and sometimes against one another for most of the thirty years of political life that still lay ahead for them all, the American faithfully supporting the Republican party while the National vigorously denounced all parties that refused to include woman suffrage in their program.

Stanton and Anthony, however, with people to the left and to the right accusing them of having sold out, were now, in the late sixties, stubbornly embattled, both feeling at this point that "it would be right and wise to accept aid from the devil himself." In January of 1868, in a letter to Thomas Higginson, who had written to admonish her for her association with George Train, Stanton explains:

Mr. Higginson, Dear Friend,

Our "pathway" is straight to the ballot box, with no variableness nor shadow of turning. I know we have shocked our old friends who were half asleep on the woman question into a new life, just waking from slumber they are cross, can't see clearly where we are going, but time will show that Miss Anthony & myself are neither idiots or lunatics . . . We do care what all good men like you *say*, but just now the men that will *do* something to help us are more important. We shall be glad to have anything from your pen either in favor or against our position, & your advice will always be received kindly & duly considered, though followed with caution & jealousy. You know the "white male" is the aristocracy of this country, we belong to the peasantry, the ruling class never did see the wrongs of the oppressed under its own heel. My cousin Gerrit Smith always laughs when I say to him that he believes in equality on a southern plantation, but not in his own home! The position of such men as Garrison, Phillips, Sumner in their treatment of our question today proves

that we must not trust any of you. All these men who have
pushed us aside for years saying "this is the negro's hour"
now when we turn from them & find help in other
quarters, turn up the whites of their eyes! & cry out the
cause.

Now let me ask, Suppose George Francis Train had
devoted his time & money for three months to the negro as
he has to the woman, would not the abolitionists on all
sides be ready to eulogize & accept him, of course they
would. Do they ignore everyone who is false to woman? By
no means. Why ask us to ignore everyone who is false to
the Negro, though Mr. T. is not when black men on the
stump & in their conventions repudiate woman? No! my
dear friend we are right in our present position. We
demand suffrage for all the *citizens of the republic* in the
Reconstruction. I would not talk of negroes or women,
but citizens; there is where Wendell Phillips failed; he
should have passed from the abolitionist to the statesman,
when slavery was abolished, instead of falling back.

The extremity was no greater than Garrison's had been over
abolition—"No union with slaveholders!"—but very few could accept the analogue. Not one of her male comrades could put himself in
her position, see the usefulness of the refusal to compromise, and
achieve the philosophical empathy that might have altered history. Garrison himself was appalled by Stanton and Anthony's association with
Train, and his sympathetic identification with them ceased on the spot.

The inability of so many intelligent women and men to grasp
the large, iconic meaning of insisting on universal suffrage and nothing but universal suffrage drove Stanton to the wall. Forced to ex-

plain herself again and again, she thought harder about *why* all compromise on this issue was doomed. In January of 1869 Lucy Stone
and her husband, Henry Blackwell, addressed a woman suffrage meeting in Washington to urge once more the submission to Congress of
two separate amendments. Stanton then spoke out even more plainly
than before, drawing on twenty years of organizing experience, to
explain why she was convinced the divided request would fail.

> We saw the experiment of two separate amendments fairly tried in
> Kansas . . . We know how the women were roused, and their settled
> hostility to the Negro breathed into the men at every hearthstone . . .
> We saw the barter on all sides of human right, Republicans pledging
> themselves to vote against the Negro, if the Democrats would vote for
> the woman, while few only, based on the broad principle of justice,
> went heartily for both propositions. The consequence was that neither
> were enfranchised.

This was one of the rare moments when she spoke as realistically
about her own sex as Mary Wollstonecraft had in *Vindication of the
Rights of Woman*. No purist she, Stanton had so often throughout the
years, especially when addressing legislatures and conventions, talked
out of both sides of her mouth about women—on the one hand
they were just like men, on the other they were never anything but
pure, virtuous, long-suffering (today's language of "sameness" and
"difference" would have been perfectly familiar to her, but today she
couldn't have gotten away with using *both*, as she so shamelessly and
indiscriminately did in her own time). Now, however, at this crucial
moment in 1869, it seemed necessary to her to speak the single,
larger truth: at stake lay the only humanist vision that would allow
her sex to rise above itself in order that it might become itself.

She observed that in political life men *act* as if they believe all men equal (especially around election time); in time the practice makes them more amenable to liberal ideas than the women who stand beside them: "The effect of concentrating all woman's thoughts and interest on home life intensifies her selfishness and narrows her ideas in every direction, hence she is arbitrary in her views of government, bigoted in religion and exclusive in society; and is ever insidiously infusing her ideas into the men by her side." We will never have a genuine republic, she goes on, until the women "are baptized into the idea" of equality, "until they understand the genius of our institutions, study the science of government and have a direct voice in our legislation." None of which can happen unless they, *together* with black men, are initiated into true citizenship through the practice of exercising the right to vote.

The campaign for universal suffrage became moot that year when Congress passed the Fifteenth Amendment, granting universal manhood suffrage. Elizabeth Stanton denounced her government as having created an "aristocracy of sex," blatantly sanctioning dominant and subordinate categories of citizenship for men and women; thereby blasting America's long, hard effort to achieve a true republic.

It was now twenty-one years since Seneca Falls. If ever there was a moment of truth for woman suffrage, this was it. Stanton and her comrades had all grown gray in service to The Cause. Not only that, but the simple solidarity of the early movement was now unhappily dissolved. That very year (1869) the National Woman Suffrage Association was founded, with Stanton as president; almost immediately, Lucy Stone formed the competing American Woman Suffrage Association. The split within the woman's movement was cemented into place. Moreover, beyond the split, the movement seemed to have been much weakened because it had honored the abolitionist request to suspend activities until the war was over. "This generous policy proved disastrous for the woman's rights cause," Stanton later wrote. "With feminist organizations disbanded, and their activities in abeyance, conservatives easily repealed feminist gains. In 1862, for example, the New York legislature rescinded most of the 1860 Married Women's Property Act, and there was little public outcry."

Now, a century later, we can see that Stanton's take on the war and the woman's movement was not really the most accurate. The feminists came out of the Civil War with far more political savvy than they had entered it, the long, harrowing dispute over universal suffrage having sharpened both wits and tactics. Nevertheless, what was required now, in 1869, was an extraordinary amount of organizing just to regain lost ground. Hundreds of women in both associations—women named Sara Spencer and Mathilde Anneke and Virginia Minor and Mary Hazlett and Hannah Comstock—threw themselves anew into suffrage work—rallies, meetings, and conventions; articles, petitions, and circulars. Stanton and Anthony themselves hit the road as they had never hit it before, traveling the lyceum circuit repeatedly, from one end of the country to the other. The 1870s was an astonishing time of renewed energy and activism that would reveal to the feminists themselves how vital a part of the century of American self-belief they had become, and how absolutely alone in it they were. For Stanton, as for every other kind of American, political time had divided itself irrevocably into Before and After the Civil War. She understood as never before how rooted was the resistance to equality for women. At the same time, it was only after the war that it was possible for her—as well as most American feminists—to see what a remarkable piece of political machinery they had been building since 1848, and how capable it was of making them stay the course.

III

1867

WE ARE ALONE

THE WOMEN'S RIGHTS CONVENTION of the 1850s was a
piece of genius. It was to nineteenth-century feminism what
consciousness-raising was to the twentieth. Within weeks of Seneca
Falls, the conventions began—first in nearby cities such as Rochester
and Philadelphia; then in the surrounding states (Connecticut, Pennsylvania, Rhode Island); and then, in 1850, the First National
Women's Rights Convention was called in Worcester, Massachusetts.

As Susan Conrad puts it in *Perish the Thought* (her admirable study
of intellectual women in nineteenth-century America), the conventions were "a moveable feast, a college and a long conversation." Just
as with consciousness-raising, these meetings allowed women-on-the-
verge to see that there was a way, out of their own experience, to make
a remarkable amount of political and social sense of how the world
had come to organize itself. Once a woman's own experience had been
established as a legitimate base from which to start an intellectual
journey, she found herself digging purposefully into history, religion,
literature, and moral philosophy, in order that she might better argue

the evidence of her senses. In no time at all, the range of subjects and speakers at these conventions expanded to include speculations that only yesterday might have been dismissed as peripheral to the question of women's rights, but with each meeting were more willingly entertained as central to an ever-expanding view of the enterprise. Had it not been for the conventions, many of the women who became crucial to the movement would never have known not only that they could think, but that there were many like themselves *out there* who could also think. Within five years, at an extraordinary number of national, state, and city meetings, American women everywhere discovered that there was intellection among women.

The correspondence that those meetings gave rise to testifies eloquently to the kind of life-giving vitality they set in motion. Not only in Stanton's letters, but in the letters of Susan Anthony, Lucy Stone, Lucretia Mott, Paulina Davis, Isabella Hooker, Martha Wright, Antoinette Brown, Angelina Grimké—letters alive with energy, color, and intelligent devotion—we find the same mixture of convention planning and family news, questions of strategy and movement gossip, positions endorsed or rejected, and accounts of life on the lecture circuit. The convention provided the purposeful, ongoing context within which they could meet and write and become themselves. It was the equivalent of all the institutions—university, workplace, office, club— that men used to enliven their being through the kind of integrated social contact that gives one back more of the self than one had before. And indeed, from the beginning there were a number of liberal-minded men cheering the conventions on. As Paulina Wright Davis, one of the organizing committee for the first national convention, wrote to Stanton in advance of the meeting: "One gentleman said to me make any demands you please upon my purse to further the object of the convention. When I asked Mr. Channing for his name, 'Yes, with all my heart' was the response, so also Mr. Alcott, Dr. Elder of Philadelphia, and many others whose names do not now occur to me."

Along with the conventions came a blizzard of writing activity—tracts, notices, circulars, and petitions—the petitions going first to the state legislatures, and then, year after year after year, to Washington. Over the years Elizabeth Stanton wrote thousands of them for the state of New York, as well as for Washington. It was here, in this grassroots activity, that her partnership with Susan Anthony found its level. Below is a typical example of how things, within two years of their meeting, were being done:

First, an announcement was placed in *Frederick Douglass's Paper*, in the *New York Semi-Weekly*, and in the feminist newspapers *Lily* and *Una*:

Seneca Falls, Dec 11, 1854

TO THE WOMEN OF THE STATE OF NEW YORK

To every intelligent, thinking woman we put the question, On what sound principles of jurisprudence, constitutional law, or human rights, are one-half of the people of this State disenfranchised? If you answer, as you must, that it is done in violation of all law, then we ask you, when and how is this great wrong to be righted? We say *now*; and petitioning is the first step in its accomplishment. We hope, therefore, that every woman in the State will sign her name to the petitions . . .

Elizabeth Cady Stanton
Chair'n N.Y. Women's Rights

A few weeks after this announcement appeared in the papers, another appeared in the *New York Daily Tribune* giving the schedule for a

93

series of New York county women's rights conventions being held
"to discuss all the reasons that impel Woman to demand her Right
of Suffrage," this one signed:

> By order of the N.Y. State Woman's Rights Committee
> Susan B. Anthony
> General Agent, Rochester, NY

After the first announcement, either Stanton or Anthony, or both,
would receive an instant response from any of a dozen feminists of
their acquaintance to acknowledge the call to action, and at the same
time give news and extend solidarity. The one below is typical:

> *Andover, Mass Dec 28, 1854*
>
> Dear Mrs. Stanton,
>
> I was very glad to know that you and Susan were taking
> hold of the work so full of energy. God bless you both . . .
> I thought from what Mrs. Rose said that she would also
> work earnestly . . . The New Englanders are looking with
> interest to see what *our state* will do.
>
> Cordially ever, Antoinette Brown

Because it *was* an age of reform, hundreds of middle-class women
joined the ranks of the protestors—they had enough company to
brave the social stigma that would otherwise have made them ignore
their own strong feeling—and by 1848, many of these women had
already been out on the road for a number of years as speakers on the
lecture circuit, traveling on behalf of temperance or abolition. They

routinely covered all of New York State, Pennsylvania, New Jersey, and New England; later, Ohio, Kansas, Iowa, and the far west— speaking repeatedly in hundreds of towns, suburbs, and villages. Now their passions shifted to include—and then be overtaken by— women's rights. As things turned out, Stanton was far from the only one whose activist life spanned fifty years. Hardly anyone ever walked away from it. Devotion to The Cause was not negotiable. Movement work simply became integrated into the pressures of daily life—a thing to be reported on, not complained of:

> Dear Elizabeth, I regret that I cannot come to Seneca Falls for the meeting as I have been sick . . . We ought early to consider where will be the best place for the next National gathering, and when the best time.

> Dear Lucy, Mrs. Stanton's baby is hardly recovered from fever & ague . . . Meanwhile Nette remains in Massachusetts where she had a severe attack of rush of blood to the head after her return from Cleveland, & has not yet fully recovered it . . . But it is necessary that the November meeting be planned . . .

> My dear Susan, A few lines to say to you how disappointed I felt, at being obliged to part so abruptly at the close of the Convention . . . the impure air of that ante room gave me such a severe head ache that I was scarcely able to do anything . . .

> My dear Mrs. Stanton, I regret that I am unable to come to Chicago—my husband being in dire financial straits, &

the entire household in turmoil—but it is absolutely
urgent that you attend . . . write . . . speak . . . cast your
vote . . .

This kind of report goes on for thirty years: births, babies, ill-
ness; household disasters large and small; husbands dead, dying, going bankrupt; depression reported as an attack of nerves or stomach
ailment or blood to the head—all endured before and after every
meeting, lecture tour, or convention, and all related in the same sto-
ical, upright, Eleanor Roosevelt voice. These complaints are never the
subject of a letter; merely a few lines inserted *out of courtesy* to the re-
cipient of the letter. If complaint there was, it was only that one
couldn't attend the meeting, go on the tour, take part in the convention. They were women who rose brilliantly to one of the deepest
excitements of their time: the national conviction that human
perfectibility was within its grasp, "bodied forth" in women's rights.
Nothing, absolutely nothing, gave them back a stronger sense of
their own expressive selves interacting with something large than the
active pursuit of suffrage for women.

Lucy Stone and Antoinette Brown were both close to Susan
Anthony in sensibility, and from the beginning theirs was a letter-
writing intimacy of remarkable openness. (What a loss Stone's
friendship must have been for Anthony!) The quality of these rela-
tionships is revealing. Lucy Stone and Nette Brown were like sisters
to Anthony; with these two she experienced an easy affection that
centered, of course, on movement work, but did not preclude girlish
confidences. Conversely, Stanton, with whom she achieved a justifi-
ably famous partnership, remained a figure of awe toward whom Anthony yearned for many years. So on the one hand, she could write
to Lucy Stone:

August 8, 1857

Dear Lucy,

I returned from [the New York State Teachers meeting in]
Binghamton Friday AM at 10:30—travelled by night to
save time&heat&dust—I have ordered the "Binghamton
Republican" sent to you & Nette from which you will get
some idea of the proceedings of the Teachers Convention.
On the whole, there is great gain—a large majority of the
Convention was on the side of justice&equality, and could
the several questions have been *fairly discussed* & voted upon,
would every one of them been carried—but the President
was so *bitter* against all reform, he *could* not *deal fairly*—for
instance, the Chair of the Committee on my "Color"
Resolutions [opposing the exclusion of black children
from the schools], sprung upon the Convention his *minority
report*—not one of us suspecting it—had kept perfectly
hush in the Committee—and he had a man ready to move
its adoption, in a twinkling, & the President put the
question while I stood on my feet crying, *Mr. President*—
thus was the cause&I cheated out of my speech—I can't
tell you anything of the *mean insulting* manner of the
president from the beginning to the end.

   Professor Davies was told to his face, by one of the
best men Teachers of the State, that his Wednesday Evening
speech was the *most villainous speech* ever made [Davies had
denounced Anthony's resolution to open all schools to
women as well as men as "the first step in that school which
sought to abolish marriage"] . . . Oh, how I did wish *you*
were there to dress him down—but I did the best I could.

97

And Antoinette Brown, on the eve of her marriage to Samuel
Blackwell in January of 1856, could write to *Anthony*:

Dearest Susan,

Can you ever forgive me? You must know I am very
penitent! . . . When we had the long talk that night at Mrs.
Stanton's . . . we talked of Sam'l C. Blackwell and [I] said
what *at the time* was felt, that I should drop the
correspondence with him entirely, which it is needless to
say now was never done. At Boston I own up to hoaxing
you and Lucy and Ellen, all of you—yet even then the
matter was not decided but was just at the crisis where it
must be decided for weal or woe at once, and I was more
than half in earnest in the proposition that you should
make his acquaintance for there were no two people that
I liked much better than both of you . . . After more than
a week's visit with him the scales predominated decidedly
in his favor. When you asked me that night in Rochester
whether I should not feel bad when "Sam was married" I
came near shaking you onto the floor with laughing at the
joke for he was in the city then and was going up to spend
the week at Father's . . .

Susan darling, I love you a little better than ever and
would ask you to the wedding only that absolutely no one
is invited, my mother's health is so feeble . . .

You may be sure of my continued interest and future
cooperation in our N.Y. movement, and in every other
good cause. I go right on with the writing, and even

lecturing some more this winter. Write me, won't you? Ever yours, Nette

Two months later Antoinette is writing again to Anthony to say that she is ready to go lecturing; then she gossips a bit about Lucy Stone, now her sister-in-law (Stone having married Sam's brother Henry), and ends with, "And for you, Sue, I hear of a number of bachelors making inquiries about Susan B. Anthony. This means something! I shall look out for another wedding before the year closes, among our sisternity. Get a good husband—that's all, dear." (Lucy Stone soon sends the same kind of letter to Anthony, "My husband would send love, but he is down at the store—I wish you had a good husband too—It is a great blessing.")

But however sisterly Anthony acted with these women, within herself she remained sealed off, painfully self-protective; she could not make sufficient connection through the senses to break her own internal solitariness. It was only to Stanton, not to either Lucy or Nette, that Anthony, in the following year, could write:

Dear Mrs. Stanton,

How I do long to be with you this very minute—to have one look into your very soul & one sound of your soul stirring voice—

I did hope to call on you before embarking on this Western voyage—but time & opportunity came not . . . I can't remember whether I have answered your last letter or not—be that as it may, I well remember how good a word it brought to me and how it cheered me onward—Mrs.

Stanton, I have *very weak moments*—and long to lay my
weary head somewhere and nestle my full soul close to that
of another in full sympathy—I sometimes fear that I *too*
shall faint by the wayside—and drop out of the ranks of
the faithful few—

There is so much, mid all that is so hopeful, to
discourage & dishearten—and I feel *alone*. Still I know I am
not alone but all the true & the good souls, both in & out of
the body, keep me company, and that the Good Father
more than all is ever a host in every good effort.

But you will see that this is *one* of my *tired moments*—so
no more—but to the Cause thereof—

Very soon after this letter she is, of course, back in harness, writing to Lucy, "I want this [next national] convention to strike *deeper*
than any of its predecessors. It seems to me we have played on the
surface of things quite long enough. Getting the right to hold property, to vote, to wear what dress we please, &c&c, are all good—but
Social Freedom, after all, lies at the bottom of all—& until woman
gets that, she must continue the slave of man in all other things."

She was intensely repressed. She was immensely decent. A remarkable exchange between herself and Ernestine Rose, recorded in
her diary, makes startlingly clear how real that decency was.

Ernestine Rose (born in 1810) was an educated Polish Jew who
left home, got herself to England, became a passionate socialist, married an English radical, and arrived in New York in 1836. A skilled
public speaker, she was soon a favorite of the American reform
movement and was, throughout the 1850s, a beloved presence on the
women's rights lecture circuit. But she never felt at home in the

United States, and after the Civil War she and her husband returned to England.

On April 9, 1854, Anthony and Rose were together in Baltimore. The entry in Anthony's diary for that day reads as follows:

Very pleasant morning. Mr. Wheadon called & accompanied us to the Universalist Church to hear a sermon on "Woman's Sphere" from Mr. Flanders. The hymns were beautiful, one verse [in particular]. The minister admitted the justice of the demand of woman for her Rights, but denied that they were identical with man's. The sermon was a bundle of inconsistencies.

Mrs. R. & myself were talking of the "*Know Nothing*" organization, when she criticized Lucy Stone & Wendell Phillips with regard to their feelings toward foreigners. Said she had heard them both express themselves in terms of prejudice against granting to foreigners the rights of Citizenship. I expressed disbelief as to either of them having that narrow, mean prejudice in their souls. She then said I was blinded & could see nor hear nothing wrong in that clique of Abolitionists. She thought she being connected with no Society or association, either in religion or reforms, could judge all impartially. I then ventured to say that she did not criticize Kossuth [the Hungarian "freedom fighter" who failed to speak out against slavery while he was in the States] as she would an American. She thought she did, & could see reasons why he pursued the course he did. Yes, said I, you excuse him because you can see the causes why he acted & spoke thus, while you will not allow me to bring forward the probable causes of Lucy's seeming fault—It seemed to *me* that *she* could not ascribe *pure motives* to any of our Reformers, while to her it seemed that I was blindly bound to see no fault, however glaring. At length in the anguish of my soul, I said, Mrs. Rose, "there is not one in the Reform ranks whom you think true, not one but whom panders to the popular feeling." She answered, I can't help it, I take them by the words of their own mouths. I trust all until their own words or acts declare them false to truth & right, and, continued she, no one can tell the hours of anguish I have suffered, as one after another I have seen those whom I had trusted, betray falsity of motive, as I have been compelled to place one after another on the list of panderers to public favor. Said I, do you know Mrs. Rose, that I can but feel that you place *me too* on that list. Said she, I will tell you, when I see you untrue. A silence ensued, while I copied the verse from the hymn sung at Church this A.M., & subscribed it Susan B. Anthony, for her dear friend Ernestine L. Rose. As I handed it to her, I observed tears in her eyes. Said I, Mrs. Rose, have I been wicked, & hurt your feelings. She answered, No, but I expect never to be understood while I live—her anguish was extreme. I too wept, for it filled my soul with anguish to see one so noble, so true (even though I felt I could not comprehend her) so bowed down, so overcome with deep swelling emotions. At length she said, no one knows how I have suffered from not being understood—I know you must suffer & heaven forbid that I should add a feather's weight to your burdens—

What Ernestine Rose was forcing on Anthony was the uncomfortable recognition that the distinguished figures of reform were not always men and women of superior moral character. Devotion to freedom for the slaves, or the rights of women, had not necessarily freed them of the many small (and sometimes large) ways in which all those not like oneself continue to seem unreal even as one is declaring that, in principle, they *are* real.

Which leads us to the now famous charge of Stanton's racism: namely, that in a number of places, both publicly and privately, she used the word "Sambo" when referring to blacks; in particular, when she realized that the Fourteenth Amendment was going to give black men the vote but not women, she wrote, in a rage, that she couldn't believe that "Sambo" was going to walk through the door before she did (she also, I might add, invariably referred to the Irish as either drunken or stupid or ignorant, and thought the uneducated—especially the immigrant uneducated—should not have the vote).

In her own time, the radicals were scandalized that Stanton would not give on "This is the negro's hour," but no one really held her accountable for the epithet "Sambo"—as throughout the years, many of us have not held ourselves or others accountable for similar verbal cruelties uttered by people passionate about righting society's wrongs. I grew up among left-wing immigrant Jews whose active devotion to social justice for the international working class was fiercely personal, as it had grown out of their own humiliated sense of outsiderness; yet, almost all of them said *schvartze* when referring to blacks and *goyim* when referring to gentiles. In their mouths these words, while ostensibly only neutral terms of description, were epithets for "not quite human like us." In short, the unreality of others is endemic—in "us" as well as in "them"—historic and endemic. When Emerson said, "We must treat all people as if they are real, because who knows? Perhaps they are," we realize that he couldn't have had the insight if he hadn't known the feeling.

That black hole of human failure is the bitterness of all our lives: the sheer, breathtaking void of the soul that is experienced when you wake up one day to realize that you yourself are not as real to the people with whom you live as they are to themselves! That moment feels profoundly humanizing; but as it turns out, it only reveals our own emotional damage. We do not wake up to such a realization saints, we wake up wounded animals. The awakening does not humanize us—on the contrary, more often than not, "they" are more "they" than ever—it is in fact only the beginning of a long, painfully slow process of self-rehabilitation. As Chekhov so memorably put it, "Others have made me a slave, but I must squeeze the slave out of myself, drop by drop."

Yet we hold on—how we hold on!—to our own damage. If we live long enough we come to understand how strangely persistent a human necessity it is to *not* let go of the unreality of a class of beings other than ourselves—at the same time that we denounce it in theory from the political rafters. The road to *actual* empathy is long and hard-going—and requires cultural change of a high order. So yes, Elizabeth Stanton felt sexism keenly, worked hard to end slavery, loved some people who were either black or Irish—and still she could say "Sambo" when angry, or "ignorant Irishman" when irritated. I think, though, that had she lived on into our own time when the civil rights movements of the sixties and seventies taught millions of us to understand—*really* understand—what it felt like to be on the other side of words and gestures that routinely discount the reality of another, she would have been among the first to be transformed.

IN 1876 IT WAS PROPOSED that a sixteenth amendment—for which many interests competed—be added to the Constitution. Elizabeth Stanton proposed that it be devoted to universal suffrage, and an extraordinary push was made by the woman's rights movement to claim it for its own.

"Senator Morton wants that amendment to declare that the people shall vote directly for president," Susan Anthony told the newspaper reporters. "Blaine wants sectarian schools not to receive state aid; the Christians want to put God in the constitution; the radicals go to the other extreme; the temperance people want the liquor traffic stopped; I protest against all this and want that amendment to enfranchise women."

Stanton issued an appeal from the National Woman Suffrage Association to all American women in which she said that the National understood that many, "out of weariness and despair, have vowed to appeal no more." Nevertheless, the organization urged "the women of this country to make now the same united effort for their own rights that they did for the slaves at the south, when the 13th Amendment was pending." After which, both she and Anthony—now in their sixties and having been at it for nearly thirty years—once again hit the road.

Between September 4, 1877, and April 18, 1878, Susan Anthony lectured 148 times on the Sixteenth Amendment in 140 towns across ten states to audiences ranging in size from forty to fifteen hundred. For each lecture delivered, Anthony received either twenty-five dollars in cash or a portion of the receipts. Tickets were fifty and seventy-five cents apiece. After she spoke she invariably took a vote on suffrage for women and almost always the crowd cheered, "Yes!" This made her report back, "The friends of our cause are nearing the millions." She knew, of course, that it was only in her presence, not necessarily later, that so many were roused to support The Cause—but the response, real or imagined, kept her going. Her diaries give us a vivid glimpse of what it meant to keep going:

In Indiana she's up at four in the morning in pouring rain, crossing a swollen river, trains and engines crashing by, when halfway across the ferryman shouts, "Train's gone!" and they must turn back. In a town in Colorado she mounts a dry-goods box on the courthouse steps "with the Rocky Mts. for the 4 walls, & the blue sky for

a roof." Another town is reached by driving fifty miles over a dangerous mountain trail, and camping out at night. Next day, a hundred
miles by buckboard over another mountain pass, then twenty-one
miles down a river, crossing the Continental Divide to reach a town
"Where nobody knew that anybody believed in Woman Suffrage."
The day after that, she arrives in the afternoon at a place where no
notice of her coming has been given, and she has "to begin at the
foundation of things, hire a hall, get dodgers printed and distributed,
etc."; by eight-thirty in the evening she has eaten supper, put on her
lace collar, and is speaking to a crowd of men, women, and children
"packed into the dining room of a hotel, the first nail of which was
driven not over thirty days before." In the morning, up again, break-
fast eaten, and aboard the stage at six a.m. speeding westward "at the
rate of eight miles an hour," arriving "weary, dusty, utterly forlorn"
but speaking that evening "in a new large M.E. church, crowded to
its utmost, and again at the close a solid 'aye' vote of both men and
women."

But such is the woman's capacity for spirit that two days later she
writes:

I took the stage for Lake City, a distance of 84 miles, rode all that
night and all the next day to 1 pm over the mountains and through
their various passes, crossing the divide between the waters that flow
into the Atlantic and Pacific—at its highest point over 11,000 feet.
And the ride down that mountain pass, "Slum Gullion" they call it,
was the most fearful rough and tumble I ever experienced, though I returned overland from Oregon to California—nearly 400 miles—in
1871, and thought I knew all in that line . . . all that fearfully long, but
beautiful, frosty night, the moon shone brightly and on scenery most

magnificent. At midnight I alighted at Wagon Wheel Gap, and with tin cup in hand trudged through the sand to the Rio Grande bank, bound to drink fresh from the pure, cold waters from the snowy peaks above. It was here, where the mountains crowd up to the river's edge so closely, that Fremont, in his early survey was compelled to leave his wagons, hence the name. The rock bound sides are not only perpendicular but actually overhanging the river thousands of feet below . . .

Stanton leaves her own paper trail behind her, one that spans the better part of the late 1870s, and traces the shameless self-praise *she* used to keep herself going, along with the unavoidable mood swings:

Chicago, February 16, 1875

Dear Susan:

I have been in Chicago for some three days and such a rush of people you never saw. I had a magnificent audience at the Grand Opera House, packed with people on the stairs, sidewalks and even out into the street . . . When I saw the crowds in the street I did feel like running! But when I was fairly launched and every eye on me, I could feel the pluck and pathos slowly rising and went through the ordeal with credit to myself and to you . . .

The people in the country towns are crazy to hear lectures . . . One night people came twenty miles to hear me . . . At this last place, the audience despaired of me [because of snow blockades] though I telegraphed I was on the way in a cutter . . . I stepped on the platform in traveling dress, but supperless, the audience, from miles around, on the spot and ready to listen. These splendid people are hungry, hungry, and I always feel that what I have to say is inadequate. Oh, for more power to give out the truth!

Ohio, March, 1877

Dear Hattie,

These trips have taught me one thing in regard to myself, and that is that I can be happy under most conditions. I see so many people fretting and discontented under the most promising circumstances that I have come to the conclusion that heaven and hell depend more on our organizations than on our environment.

Missouri, Spring, 1879

Dear Libby,

Two months more containing sixty one days still stretch their long length before me. I must pack and unpack my trunk sixty one times, pull out the black silk trail and don it, curl my hair, and pin on the illusion [lace] puffing round my spacious throat, sixty one more times, rehearse my lecture sixty one times, eat 183 more miserable meals, sleep in cotton sheets with these detestable things called "comforters" (tormentors would be a more fitting name) over sixty one more nights, shake hands with sixty one more committees, smile, look intelligent and interested in every one who approaches me, while I feel like a squeezed sponge . . .

But a month later in Nebraska, to her three sisters in New York:

I am a wonder to every one for my endurance and cheerfulness. Comparing myself with most women, I have come to the conclusion that I was well born, that my parents put me together with unusual wisdom and discretion, for which I am devoutly thankful. I enjoy life under the most adverse circumstances and am in no particular hurry to be translated.

An entry in her diary during this time gives an even better idea of how many, out there, must have experienced *her*:

A burly son of Adam escorted me to the passenger car filled with German immigrants, with tin cups, babies, bags, and bundles innumerable. The ventilators were all closed, the stoves hot, and the air was like that of the Black Hole of Calcutta. So, after depositing my cloak and bag in an empty seat, I quietly propped both doors open with a stick of wood, shut up the stoves, and opened all the ventilators with the poker. But the celestial breeze, so grateful to me, had the most unhappy effect on the slumbering exiles. Paterfamilias swore outright; the companion of his earthly pilgrimage said, "We must be going north," and, as the heavy veil of carbolic acid gas was lifted from infant faces, and the pure oxygen filled their lungs and roused them to new life, they set up one simultaneous shout of joy and gratitude, which their parents mistook for agony. Altogether here was a general stir. As I had quietly slipped into my seat and laid my head down to sleep, I remained unobserved— the innocent cause of the general purification and vexation.

Purification and vexation, indeed. That should have gone on her tombstone.

By May she was near exhaustion. Urged by Susan B. to attend the national meeting taking place in St. Louis, she writes from Iowa,

> I have such a crick in my back that the least motion distresses me. I rode thirty miles yesterday across the prairies in a stiff wind and took cold. This, added to the lameness I have had in my back ever since my [cart and horse] upset, makes me feel very low spirited. Unless I am better tomorrow I shall give up my Little Sioux appointment for the 6th. I have an engagement at Cairo, Illinois, the 10th, and a dozen engagements afterward on my way home. I cannot go through the St. Louis convention. I feel as if one more ounce of responsibility would kill me. I am sick, tired, jaded beyond description . . .

In the end, of course, she *did* go to St. Louis, although by now she was heartily sick of the meetings and had begun dreading them long before their actual arrival dates. In October of 1874 she had written to Martha Wright, "Do you know I am so nervous at the very thought of a convention that I count the months, weeks & days before its approach, just as used to do the advent of the various men children I have brought into the world. It is such a task to make them run smoothly, to fill up the time with *good speaking*, to choke bores . . . I am always racked with anxiety." And then again, in December, to Antoinette Blackwell, "Our speakers all seem so thin and feeble, compared with the glowing eloquence of all classes of men under similar oppression . . . I hope & pray Susan does not propose to march us all to Washington this winter [actually, it was New York this time]. These biennial attacks are too much . . ."

In this same letter Stanton cheers herself up with a malicious bit of gossip: "The richest thing [Lucy Stone's] *Woman's Journal* has said in many a day, is Lucy & Blackwell having rescued the woman move-

ment from the disgrace into which the rest of us had dragged it.
What a blessing! It was worth while for the little Englishman to
come three thousand miles to do so grand a thing." This is a reference
to the Beecher-Tilton scandal of 1872. Victoria Woodhull, the flam-
boyantly problematic feminist known far and wide as a defender of
"free love," had been the one to let the newspapers know that the famous preacher was sleeping with his married parishioner. Woodhull
was then blasted by Beecher's defenders (among them Stone and
Blackwell), but Stanton and Anthony had refused to join in the attack. "Women have crucified the Mary Wollstonecrafts, the Fanny
Wrights, and the George Sands of all ages," Stanton said at the time.
"If this present woman must be crucified, let men drive the stakes."
The National Woman Suffrage Association was then branded by its
enemies as the party of "free love"—from which, Lucy Stone was
now concluding, the whole movement had to be rescued.

This weariness of mind as well as body was, oddly enough, both
compounded and, at the same time, mitigated by the growing knowledge that the world was heartily tired of her cause: not tired enough
to stop contesting the justice of its demands, simply tired of being
forced to hear them rehearsed year after year. Nothing made Stanton
flare more quickly than being told that women's rights had become
boring. Just before the May 1875 convention, a letter from London,
published in a New York journal, complained that in a recent address
by suffragists before the House of Commons "the same old arguments were made to do duty once more." In an article called "Nothing New" Stanton replied hotly:

> Why, in discussing fundamental principles of human rights, should
> woman be expected, like a kaleidoscope, to present an endless variety
> of views to subjects that men present in the same old way . . .

I notice that men—white, black, foreign and native—in all their
convocations—political, religious, reformatory, commercial, educa-
tional, agricultural, social, and scientific—say the same old things their
fathers said before them. But the press reports them, one and all, re-
spectfully, without ever telling the world that these same old men met
together and said the same old things . . .

In the debate on self government in Louisiana last year [we had]
the same old arguments on "states rights" . . . and not one criticism
was made on the . . . lack of novelty in their arguments . . .

In noticing the ups and downs of the stock market . . . reporters
do not say that the same old men gathered in the exchange, and made
themselves princes and paupers in the same old way . . .

But [when it comes to] woman suffrage, instead of giving the
public a new interest in finding out woman's true status before the law,
they blame the movement for the transient darkness instead of the
chance meteor passing between it and the sun.

Whatever the day or the hour brought—hope, despair, exhilara-
tion, fury—Stanton always had a passion of words at her command
with which to make sense, and endow meaning. Invigorated in July of
1878, she addresses a Seneca Falls anniversary meeting with a clear
heart:

Looking back over the past thirty years how long ago seems that July
morning when we gathered round the altar in the old Wesleyan Church
in Seneca Falls. It taxes and wearies the memory to think of all the
conventions we have held, the calls, the resolutions we have penned, the
never ending debates we have kept up in public and private, and yet to
each and all our theme is as fresh and absorbing as it was the day we
started . . . In this struggle for justice we have deepened and broadened

our own lives, and extended the horizon of our vision . . . The past to all of us is filled with regrets. We can recall social ambitions disappointed, fond hopes wrecked, ideals in wealth, power, position, unattained, much that would be considered success in life unrealized. But . . . the energy we have devoted to the freedom of our countrywomen, that insofar as our lives have represented this great movement, the past brings us only unalloyed satisfaction.

Yet, six months later, she is in an unholy rage. Giving the opening speech in Washington at NWSA's Eleventh Convention (January 11, 1878) she erupts:

In less than sixty days the 45th Congress will have passed into history. What shall we find on its pages concerning women? . . . That the Senate Committee on Privileges and Elections gave *three minutes* to [our petitions]! At the close of the session, and at the close of the day, in the twilight hour, when even bats and owls begin to see clearly . . . *three minutes* of consideration, two of which might have been consumed in the roll call, and the third in awaiting the arrival of the tardy chairman, this committee of the highest legislative body in the land, voted down the woman suffrage resolution 6 to 3 . . .

It was to this Congress that she had delivered, three days earlier, an immensely detailed speech of which she afterward said, "I never felt more exasperated than on this occasion [when I had to endure] the studied inattention and contempt of the chairman, Senator Wadleigh of New Hampshire . . . It was with difficulty that I restrained the impulse more than once to hurl my manuscript at his head."

And it was in this speech that, for the first time, she used the phrase "National Protection for National Citizens." In women's rights, this is the origin of what has come to be known as citizenship theory, a frame of reference used to this very day by feminist social theorists whose arguments reflect to a startling degree the ones used by Stanton on that January day in 1878.

The argument that Stanton made before the Senate Committee on Privileges and Elections was that the immunities and privileges of American citizenship are national in character, superseding the authority of the individual states; that nowhere does the Constitution give the states the right to deprive any citizen of the elective franchise; that the Constitution expressly declares that no state shall make or enforce any law that shall abridge the privileges or immunities of citizens; and that as the states clearly have no right to deprive naturalized citizens of the franchise, among whom women are expressly included, they certainly have no right to deprive native-born women citizens of this right.

In a letter to Matilda Gage written a year later, after the St. Louis convention, Stanton wrote, "Looking over the proceedings and resolutions, the thought struck me that the National Woman Suffrage Association is the only organization that has steadily maintained the doctrine of Federal power, against state rights." And so it was. She went on arguing, year after year after year, citing texts, sources, authorities—enduring the hopeless circularity of going to the Congress which sent her to the courts which remanded her to the states—making an appeal to American constitutional law that would never carry the day until the women's movement itself created such a force of urgency that "overnight" the Law would suddenly "see" that the right to woman suffrage had, after all, been inscribed therein all the time.

Yet their numbers did not multiply fast enough. Urged to plan a protest meeting on the nation's centennial in 1876, Susan B. wrote to Mathilde Anneke in September of 1875, "Your idea of an address to the People signed by 2 or 3 millions—would be splendid . . . but if signed by only a few thousands it would seem weak—I have very little hope or faith in our women rolling up an immense list of names for their own freedom—if we wanted them to do the Herculean task for negro men—Irish men or any class of the superior sex—they would all, as one earnest woman, rush to the work . . . [Our own women speakers] seem so listless—it is hard to keep in the patience with them."

The suffragists were now more alone than ever. "Nothing New" had addressed a pervasive mood of moral exhaustion. Early in 1879 the state and local suffrage associations went ahead anyway with the annual petition drive for Washington. The petitions were gathered, assorted, counted, rolled up; and then a group of women appeared on the floor of the House, at the moment of adjournment, to give each member a petition from his own state. Susan Anthony, who did not want to discourage a new generation of working feminists, took part in this action, although she knew it was a doomed effort, and was embarrassed when she found herself before George Hoar, the Republican congressman from Massachusetts. She apologized for the intrusion, and was deeply touched when Hoar, a longtime champion of women's rights, just as embarrassed, begged her to believe that "I hope, Madame, yet to see you on this floor, in your own right, and in business hours too."

IV

1894–2004

FROM THERE TO HERE

It is humiliating for a woman of my years to stand up
before men twenty years younger, and ask them for the
privilege of enjoying my rights as a citizen in a Republic.
I feel that I can never do it again.

A T THE END OF THE WOMEN'S RIGHTS convention in 1879
Stanton spoke on the floor of the St. Louis Merchants' Exchange to a thousand traders who, to her great delight, had stopped work to hear her ask for the simple right of self-government; but on the following evening, to her even greater delight, she addressed *four* thousand people at the Union Methodist Church—these numbers! Henry Beecher's Plymouth Church in Brooklyn held three thousand— where her subject was "The Bible and Woman Suffrage." After this speech a Unitarian minister in the audience invited her to address the Free Religious Society in Providence when she next came to speak at the annual meeting of the Rhode Island Woman Suffrage Association. As soon as Stanton got home to her large, lovely house across the river from Manhattan in Tenafly, New Jersey (the Stantons had been living in or around New York City since the early sixties), she wrote to the Unitarian minister, confirming her acceptance of the in-

vitation and telling him that it made her glad to find liberal thinkers
in the church, as

> the greatest block in the way of our woman suffrage movement is the
> hold the priesthood have on the women. "Thus saith the Lord" sent
> widows to the funeral pyre, hold women in harems today, Mormon
> girls in polygamy, & all women in their church pews while men preach
> their subjection, their curse, their creation as an afterthought, for man's
> happiness. And yet how difficult it is to get women out of the old
> grooves of thought; religious prejudices are stronger than all others.

It was a sentiment she had repeated many times over the years,
but it was only now, in her mid sixties, that the meaning of her own
words began to penetrate her thought anew, and command the central territory of reawakened conviction; only now that she was concentrated on how powerfully internalized, and far-reaching, was the
ritual religiosity of every American's frame of reference. She might,
in fact, have used her own bifurcated self to illustrate the insight.

In many ways, what Stanton said at the Methodist Church in St.
Louis was a demonstration of the corruption of thought and feeling
that had, from its inception, marked the long struggle in republican
America between religion and secularism, Christian thinkers and
Freethinkers. The language of Christian rhetoric was so deeply em-
bedded in the consciousness of every nineteenth-century reformer
that it was impossible to frame one's objection to the social inequities condoned by Christian dogma without using Christian rhetoric itself to describe what reform would accomplish. For example,
at Seneca Falls in 1848 Lucretia Mott delivered an address on
women's rights—described as "one of the most eloquent, logical and
philosophical discourses ever listened to"—in which she urged each

reformer present to "be as the Jesus of the present age." That same day Stanton said, "Woman has too long rested satisfied in the circumscribed limits which corrupt customs and a perverted application of the Scriptures have marked out for her." It was time for her to "move into the enlarged sphere which her great Creator has assigned her."

In this 1879 speech in St. Louis, Stanton was still speaking the language of the Christian reformer while delivering the judgment of the Freethinker: "[T]he spirit and principles of the Bible teach justice, mercy and equality," she began, but "narrow minds uniformly dwell on the letter and misquote and misapply isolated texts of Scripture, to turn this Magna Charta of human rights into an engine of oppression."

Anyone who reads the Bible correctly, she continues, will see that insofar as God is concerned women were certainly meant to take their place beside men in the world enterprise as "representative women have in all ages and nations walked outside the prescribed limits and done what they had the capacity to accomplish, and the women of the Bible form no exception. They preached, prayed, prophesied, expounded principles of government to kings and rulers, led armies, saved nations and cities by their wisdom and diplomacy, conquered their enemies by intrigue as well as courage." Yet, every movement for progress, including this one, has been compelled to come up against the objection, "The Bible is opposed to it." The defenders of slavery quoted the Bible: "Servants obey your masters." The opponents of improved working conditions quoted the Bible: "The poor ye will always have with you." And those who fight woman suffrage, simply repeat "The Bible is opposed to it." A travesty, Stanton cries. And if not a travesty—now blood begins to fill her head—an abomination. Once, at the height of the anti-slavery struggle, Frederick Douglass had said: "Prove to me that the Bible sanctions slavery, and in the name of God and humanity I would, if possible, make a bonfire of every Bible in the universe." She now echoes that heartbroken threat: "Prove that the Bible sanctions and teaches the universal subjection of woman to man as a principle of social order, and we should be compelled to repudiate its authority and do all in our power to weaken its hold on popular thought." But—slowly, the blood recedes—she does not think it will come to that because she "cannot believe that a God of law and order . . . could have sanctioned a social principle so calamitous in its consequences as investing in one-half the race the absolute control of all the rights of the other."

Whichever way the speech goes, the similes, the metaphors, the figures of speech remain Christian. "Perverted application of the Scriptures" was a phrase that would resonate in her for years. At the same time she repeatedly—and again throughout most of her life—used phrases like "her great Creator"; referred to suffrage as woman's "sacred" right to the elective franchise; and invoked the Christian euphemism for women, "purity and virtue," in nearly every speech. Consciously, Stanton was a thoroughgoing Freethinker, but, just as all nineteenth-century novelists, however sophisticated their social and psychological thought, used the conventions of melodrama in fiction, so did all public figures, including Stanton, continue to use the rhetoric of religious culture until the end of the century, and well beyond.

In the beginning, Stanton really *meant* "perverted application," implying that they, the reformers, were the *true* religious calling for the rescue of high-minded original intent from a corrupt institution run by self-serving men. "Let woman live *first* for God," she said shortly after Seneca Falls, "and she will not make imperfect man an object of reverence and idolatry." As the years progressed, however, her focus had begun ineluctably to shift. Instead of chastising the Church for having distorted the nobility of its own Book of Wisdom, she felt more and more compelled to challenge the Book itself as a collection of morality tales written by ignorant and fearful men determined on the status quo. She came to see that the Bible itself *had* instructed men from time immemorial to see women as inferior by nature—it wasn't that the Bible *served* patriarchy, the Bible *was* patriarchy—and she came to hate both established religion and the Good Book with a visceral hatred second to none.

Once Stanton came to the conclusion that the Bible was the enemy, her native radicalism kicked in: the newly enlightened heart "hardened" once again, and she gave herself over entirely to the single powerful insight that now became her light in the tunnel. (It was around this time that she said, "I am in the sunset of life and I feel it to be my special mission to tell people what they are not prepared to hear.") None of the Bible's redeeming elements—neither its poetry, nor its sympathy for human suffering, nor its necessary comfort in the face of nothingness—could alter the fact that, for her, it had become the instrument of a Faustian bargain. Only the worst kind of isolation could result from refusing to see things as they were ("the solitude of ignorance, ah who can measure its misery!"). If we believe that the purpose of life is to know the world as it is, to experience to the full the only lives that we have, in a country that fought a bitter fight to proclaim that concept a major political value—"life, liberty, and the pursuit of happiness"—then we must forgo the costly panacea of religious faith: the Will of God can never serve the Rights of Man.

Seven years after St. Louis, Stanton said flatly, "We can make no impression on men who accept the theological view of woman as the

author of sin, cursed of God, and all that nonsense. The debris of
the centuries must be cleared away before an argument for equality
can have the least significance on them."

She was set on her course. She could now recognize and endorse
what had grown painfully evident to her over the many years since
Seneca Falls—that feminism, in its very essence, was a secular movement: the one most driven, in her time, to making the republic deliver
not on an abstraction positing God's mission in America, but on another dedicated to its own worldly ideals. Organized religion was the
complicated force of reaction that women would have to break
through if they were ever to set eyes on the glorious simplicity of political equality. She would begin the effort herself with a work of
scholarship demonstrating beyond argument that Christianity was
"an old and worn-out theology full of bigotry and prejudice" and
that the overriding spirit of the Bible was, in essence and in sum,
"unfriendly to women all through."

In the summer of 1886 Stanton, her daughter Harriot (now living in England but home for a visit), and an English friend of Harriot's sat down together in the beautiful house in Tenafly to discuss
Stanton's plan for a project she called *The Woman's Bible*. The idea was
to extract from the Bible all references to women, arrange them in order, and submit them to scholarly commentary. Toward this end, the
three began by purchasing a number of cheap Bibles, cutting them
up, and pasting the relevant passages into a large scrapbook, in preparation for distribution among the right respondents. At the end of
the summer all that remained was to collect the respondents themselves.

Stanton was turned down by nearly every educated woman she
approached—scholars, linguists, anthropologists; liberal and conservative alike. "The woman's movement now included both Freethought

rationalists and evangelicals," Kathi Kern tells us in *Mrs. Stanton's Bible*, "believers in spirit and believers in matter; and a few who held that religion was no longer a significant factor in woman's emancipation." Yet all drew back, startled, from even the suggestion of such a work. What it threatened was nothing less than cultural revolution: all they wanted was the vote. Besides—this with a shrug—even though it would never do to *say* so, what the Bible said about women was not an urgent matter for suffragists.

By 1886, the cause of woman suffrage had become if not popular at least respectable. An intelligent, good-looking woman of the middle classes who worked for the vote no longer had to fear the stigma of caricature, as she would have in the years before and after the Civil War. She could now be experienced as lovely even if strong-minded, her work in the movement posing no real threat to her primary duties as a matron in society. The majority of the women running the NWSA in the eighties and nineties were competent and briskly pragmatic: they knew how to organize, develop political ties, form coalitions, exert influence on men of power. Individually, their social and political predilections ranged from the conservative to the liberal, but never approached the visionary. Although still twenty-five years away from achieving suffrage, in a sense they knew that victory was, very nearly, within the grasp of this newest generation. They were genuinely horrified at the thought of *The Woman's Bible*, not because they were necessarily believers themselves—for a significant number of Americans religion, in the last decades of the century, was not an inner reality—but the book would act as a red flag before a bull. One might ignore the dictates of Christianity in private life, but to speak out against them—in any arena of public life—was to court political disaster.

Adding to the problem was—a painful complication of the time—the fact that Christianity as a moral force *was* in trouble. The great reform movements, as well as the 1859 publication of Darwin's *On the Origin of Species*, had altered the shared sensibility more profoundly than was popularly understood and left millions of people psychologically stranded, inclining many of them not toward agnosticism but toward spiritualism—that is, a belief in communion with the dead. When in crisis, thousands found themselves unable to retreat into the Christian simplicity of God is Love, yet equally unable to go forward into the cold excitement of science and secularism. So they sat stock still, extending their hands around the séance table, praying with eyes wide shut that this intolerable littleness to which life had brought them wasn't, couldn't, be all that there was. The list of famous and accomplished men and women who, in the 1890s, subscribed to spiritualism is nothing short of remarkable.

Then, beyond—above or below—the morbid urge toward spiritualism were the many women opposed to suffrage who genuinely felt that women were genetically endowed with what the nineteenth century called "natural piety." Their numbers were legion, and they had spent their lives manipulating the idea of their own inborn morality to achieve some measure of power. Worshipping at the altar of difference—"Holy Scripture inculcates a different, and for us higher, sphere apart from public life"—they were the last on earth willing or able to take a critical look at the bargain such convictions had allowed them to strike. If some people chose to interpret woman's difference as proof that her secondary status was divinely ordained, well, that was *their* problem. When Elizabeth Stanton said, No, it's not their problem, it's your problem, these women pursed their lips and turned away from her.

At long last Stanton put together an advising committee of thirty; out of the thirty, only a handful wrote the commentaries; of the handful, Stanton herself did the majority of the work. The project took nine years to complete. It was published in two parts, in 1895 and 1898. The reviews, predictably, were not only negative, they were beside themselves with denunciation. The newspapers declared it a work of moral poison, and within the woman's movement itself repudiation was almost uniform. Lucy Stone was now dead, but her widower, Henry Blackwell, attacked *The Woman's Bible* in print within months of its publication and—what hurt the most—Stanton's own National Women's Suffrage Association publicly declared the book harmful to its cause.

Publication of *The Woman's Bible* was, for Stanton, the beginning, not the conclusion, of her last great effort to understand how women had come to be as they were. No longer made apoplectic by rejection, she now sat down to spend her few remaining years—she died in 1902—thinking about women and religion. Susan B. had argued with her in the late eighties, insisting that once women got the vote the hold that religious superstition had on them would evaporate. No, Stanton had replied, it was the other way around. The more she had read in the Bible the more persuaded she had become that women must be freed of religion *before* suffrage could do them any good. Margaret Fuller had been right when she had said, so long ago, that the vote was not the real problem in woman's life. Stanton could see now that the anxiety over equality for women went much deeper than any of them had realized.

All modern religions mythicize a Great Chain of Being in which Man is to God as Woman is to Man: in God resides the completeness of all that humanity conceives of as great and good; in man re-

sides the partialness of one equipped only to *struggle* toward the great
and the good; in woman resides all that is retarding. Man's endowment includes the necessary richness of intellectual expression and
philosophic longing; woman's portion is the weak-mindedness, the
unresolved will, devotion to the material not the transcendent.
Among Jews, Muslims, and Christians equally, man is posited as
spirit and woman as matter: she is a creature without a soul, an incarnation of sensual reduction.

Stanton had long understood religion as a mythmaking response
to all in oneself that felt weak, dirty, out of control; clearly, the need
to apportion *these* traits to one part of the race, and *those* to the other,
addressed an acuteness of mental suffering shared by women and
men alike. Now, however, she saw something else as well. She saw
that this notion of the division of traits between the sexes had become so central to the story we tell ourselves of who we are, and how
we came to be, that everything under the sun had been given a masculine or a feminine character—including the relationship between
God and his believers. Ineluctably, these characterizations had acquired a sexually charged personality. Thus, the "feminine" in human
nature—that is, the devotional—was given the task of worshipping
the "masculine" in God, and women had, in the most encompassing
sense, come to internalize the love of Jesus out of an erotic attraction
rooted in a set of emotions that could never be named for what they
were. Religion, Stanton now understood, was the dirty little secret:
an inner atmosphere of nervous excitement and primeval longing to
which one succumbed for the shuddering pleasure of coupling with
mystery. When these equations came clear, Stanton herself stood
amazed before the monumental difficulty they presented for freeing
women from what she and Anthony had so cavalierly called religious

superstition. Walk away from all that these words did not even begin to address? Just for citizenship? You'd have to be an odd woman, indeed. To this day, you'd have to be an odd woman.

ONE EVENING SOME MONTHS AGO I took a walk through the city with an old acquaintance of mine: a novelist now in her mid seventies, European-born but, having lived in the States for more than fifty years, an imaginative and talented speaker of English; also intensely Jewish, devoted to family, and well connected to New York literary life. When we first met some twenty-odd years ago—her name is Elsa—I tried to become her friend. At the time I was myself divorced and childless, a journalist at a counterculture newspaper, on the barricades for radical feminism; but we both taught writing, lived intimately with literature, exhibited the same knowing mixture of urban provincialisms, and I thought it possible that this knot of commonalities would be enough to make a connection. As things turned out, it wasn't. The years passed. We'd run into each other only occasionally. Each time, I'd feel my own puzzled sense of failure reflected in the expression I thought I saw on Elsa's face: Who *are* you? Why can't we *know* one another?

Now we met again, thrown together at a book party where the noisy chitchat bored each of us, and we were both amused to soon hear one say impulsively, "Let's get out of here," and the other nod eagerly, "Yes!" It was a soft spring evening. Finding ourselves on a street close to the East River, we decided to walk across town, back to the west side where we still both belonged.

As we walked, we spoke giddily of how estranged each of us felt these days from the world of publication parties; equally grateful, I thought, to be exchanging an opinion that was a comfort rather than a challenge. Then Elsa, in the friendliest voice, said, "Tell me, what are you working on?" I told her that I'd been writing about Elizabeth Stanton and feminism in America.

"This feminism," she said. "Tell me. What is it? What is it that you want? I don't think I've ever understood . . ."

The question startled me—I felt thrown back twenty years—but it seemed so genuinely meant that I began to talk. Elsa was a superb listener, and soon the words were pouring out of me. In fact, avenue by avenue, I was talking my whole book at her.

Suddenly, she stopped walking. She stood on the pavement, staring at me. She said, in a voice filled with something like wonderment, "You have a passion for equality."

I was so astonished that I said, "Don't you?"

"No," Elsa said, "I don't."

It was my turn to stare.

"I have a passion for many other things," she said. "For love, and friendship. For good conversation. For living inside another's imagination." She cocked her head, as though listening for the sound of her own thought. "But not for equality," she said. "There are many things I cannot live without before I cannot live without equality." She peered at me, again with that look of wonder on her face. "But not you. You, I believe, cannot live without it."

It was as though she was seeing me clearly for the first time. The strange thing was, I felt as though I, too, was seeing me "clearly" for the first time.

"No," I said. "I can't."

I don't think I had ever, until that moment, spoken these words to myself.

Then I surprised myself further. "That's what makes me one of the Odd Women."

Elsa looked puzzled.

"Every fifty years or so," I explained, "the world renames women like me—we're called the New Women, the Free Women, the Liberated Women. But George Gissing got it exactly right. He called us the Odd Women."

So we stood there, one spring night early in the twenty-first century, on the corner of Sixth Avenue and Nineteenth Street in New York City, two women—one in her sixties, the other in her seventies—staring directly into the true nature of an old divide that we ourselves embodied, and I thought I could see in her face what I was sure must be visible in mine: the thrill of realizing anew that temperament, in all its astonishing variation, makes history.

MY GENERATION OF AMERICAN FEMINISTS has discovered, with more pain and profit than any previous generation in history, how hard it is to build feminism from the inside out. Now that women have gained enough presence in the world so that millions of us are able, as never before, to know the freedom of money, education, and sexual experience, we see how *few* approach with a wholeness of mind and heart the prospect of equality for women. Those few include some men as well as some women, while the remaining majority, obviously, include most women as well as most men. The internal divide runs deep. Inequality, the radical feminists said flatly, is intolerable: if a situation is intolerable, it is not to be tolerated. Even in the late sixties, one hundred and twenty years after Seneca Falls, for all too many women as well as men, this simple equation still meant going to war with the culture. To those of us of the narrowed gaze and the hardened heart, it just meant becoming republicans with a small "r."

The similarity between Elizabeth Stanton's generation of rebels and mine remains striking. We, like them, were overtaken by the same flash of "original" insight: startled awake out of a less than grown-up dream of life to realize that men did not consider us fellow creatures; then even more startled to find that, in the main, women themselves did not sufficiently object to their subordinate position in the worldly scheme of things. To struggle for equality meant risking the comfort and reassurance of a stability that had long been in place. Our radicalism lay in declaring the risk well worth taking: a calculation almost no society as a whole is ever willing to act on; it must be driven to it. Those of us who said—and kept on saying—that the inequality of women is intolerable were perceived as, well, odd: fanatics staring with a political gaze that could not be deflected into a vision of the future that could not be achieved. When was the last time anyone had known a woman with a political gaze that could not be deflected? She was not within living memory. And for good reason. The anxiety she spread, each and every time around, was most unwelcome.

That anxiety was a dilemma we ourselves could appreciate—relaxing into all the old ways was a recurrent temptation—but we had undergone what felt like baptism by fire; we could no longer live with ourselves and accommodate a view of life that subscribed to the old arrangement between women and men. Even if we wanted to, we couldn't; the change felt organic (densely layered) and, somehow, historically commanding: its revelations daily unfolding, one beneath the other. The insistent, unyielding expectation of equality—once we were conscious of its absence—did indeed seem to mark us as American; but, as it turned out, the steady, weight-bearing loneliness to which one might be consigned in *pursuit* of the expectation—that, too, began to seem American. It was *this* development—the sheer surprise of it!—that, more than anything else, threw us back on our own history and proceeded to bind us to the culture as we had not been bound before.

The seventies was a complicated time. On the one hand, our numbers multiplied steadily, our press coverage was immense, and our presence an influence on dissenting women the world over. Yet, the all-encompassing change in American life that we had envisioned did not, of course, occur, and we could see that by continuing to *insist*, without prevailing, we might very well soon become the social eccentricity that the suffragists had been reduced to. I remember, even then, many dinner parties in small cities and university towns where I could see that radical feminism was greeted as an alarming development, and it took courage to speak out strongly. Here one did not have the privilege, as we in the urban centers did, of turning easily from those who gave us grief to those who gave us sustenance; here, one endured inner isolation in the dominant presence of one's potentially excluding familiars. Which, of course, made perfect sense. After all, as Stanton had once said, "The vast majority accept the conditions into which they are born while those who demand larger liberties are ever a small, ostracized minority." Why not suffer the established fate of the social rebel?

What was interesting, though, and what struck many of us even then, was that American feminists seemed equipped to endure the internal exile to which the dissenting view might consign one. It was as though they had tapped into something native to the culture that now, all at once, both claimed and fortified them.

In the sixties I remember watching thousands of young white people go south to discover what it meant to be black in this country; becoming radicalized, they returned home, many of them, to break with their liberal parents who opposed extreme action. The move was both thrilling and shocking: soon the country seemed filled with purposeful estrangement. Ultimately, these people helped shape one of history's great liberation movements.

In the eighties, I was struck by Israel's failure to form a significant peace movement among its dissident young, and felt puzzled as well as disturbed by the failure. But one night in New York, at a public lecture, the Israeli novelist David Grossman addressed this very question, and then I understood. He spoke alternately with calm and agitation, as though trying to explain something to himself, and then burst out, "We cannot bear to alienate ourselves from our parents." Everyone in the room could feel his anxiety. In that moment I understood my own country better.

America had *not* been built on the bedrock of the family. In America, the ethos of self-creation had fostered a proud, prickly, adolescent inclination to retreat into what is often experienced as useful solitariness. In a country like Israel, such solitariness makes people go to pieces. But here's the paradox: that famous American loneliness, with its fierce credo of self-reliance, has, time and again, become a source of collective dissident strength. It allows us to stay the course of alienation when a protracted action is required to fulfill the (broken) promise of inclusiveness into which the country was born.

And that, I believe, is why feminism is American.

When Elizabeth Stanton spoke of the solitude of self in 1892, she could not know that she had a tiger by the tail. She saw that women and men are isolated within themselves through a sense of shame that is native to humanity; she also saw the sadness and pathos of that isolation mirrored in the rooted resistance to social change ("the solitude of ignorance"); but I do not think she saw that in

America that humiliated loneliness, common to the race, would be put to great and good use in service to liberation movements in general, and the cause of women's rights in particular. Nevertheless, she more than glimpsed what lay ahead, and it is because she saw so much, and went so far in her thoughts, that we, as a generation, were able to understand as well as we did what we were living through.

BIBLIOGRAPHICAL NOTE

THIS BOOK IS NOT A WORK OF SCHOLARSHIP; nonetheless, a fair amount of reading was required in order for it to come into existence. First and foremost, of course, there was Elizabeth Cady Stanton's work itself—her speeches, letters, diaries, and autobiography:

DuBois, Ellen Carol, ed. *Elizabeth Cady Stanton/Susan B. Anthony: Correspondence, Writings, Speeches.* New York: Schocken Books, 1981.

Gordon, Ann D., ed. *The Selected Papers of Elizabeth Cady Stanton and Susan B. Anthony.* 3 vols. New Brunswick, N.J.: Rutgers University Press, 1997, 2000, 2003.

Stanton, Elizabeth Cady. *Eighty Years and More: Reminiscences, 1815–1897.* Boston: Northeastern University Press, 1992.

———. *The Woman's Bible.* New York: Arno Press, 1972.

Stanton, T., and H. Blatch, eds. *Letters, Diaries, Etc.* New York: Harper & Bros, 1922.

Then, in order to acquaint myself more fully with the outline of Stanton's political activism and the details of her intimate life, there were the biographies:

Banner, Lois. *Elizabeth Cady Stanton: A Radical for Women's Rights.* Boston: Little, Brown, 1980.
Griffin, Elizabeth. *In Her Own Right: The Life of Elizabeth Cady Stanton.* Oxford: Oxford University Press, 1985.
Lutz, Alma. *Created Equal: A Biography of Elizabeth Cady Stanton, 1815–1902.* New York: The John Day Company, 1940.

For a stronger sense of the social and political atmosphere in which Stanton grew to maturity:

Conrad, Susan P. *Perish the Thought.* Oxford: Oxford University Press, 1976.
Delbanco, Andrew. *The Real American Dream.* Cambridge, Mass.: Harvard University Press, 1999.
Foner, Eric. *The Story of American Freedom.* New York: Macmillan, 1998.
Howe, Irving. *The American Newness.* Cambridge, Mass.: Harvard University Press, 1986.
Jehlen, Myra. *American Incarnation.* Cambridge, Mass.: Harvard University Press, 1989.
Morgan, Edmund S. *American Slavery, American Freedom.* New York: W. W. Norton, 1975.
Richardson, Robert D. *Emerson: The Mind on Fire.* Berkeley: University of California Press, 1996.
Stanley, Amy. *From Bondage to Contract.* Cambridge: Cambridge University Press, 1998.

And, at last, the rereading of one of the works of feminist scholarship that has meant the most to me:

Okin, Susan Moller. *Women in Western Political Thought.* Princeton: Princeton University Press, 1979.

Printed in the USA
CPSIA information can be obtained
at www.ICGtesting.com
LVHW091146150724
785511LV00005B/562

9 780374 530563